# THE TROUBLE WITH RACIAL RECONCILIATION

# THE TROUBLE WITH RACIAL RECONCILIATION

Why John Perkins' Theological Approach Works

By

KENNETH N. YOUNG

**THE TROUBLE WITH RACIAL RECONCILIATION**



ISBN: 978-0-911802-23-8

Published in the United States of America
by
**NextStep Resources**
7890 12th Ave South Minneapolis, MN 55425
(800) 444-2665

Cover Concept: Stephen L Young Design
Design, Layout and Format: Kim Gardell, Graphic Design

# CONTENTS

# PREFACE

This book presents the work of John Perkins in conversation with other black theologians in order to lay the groundwork for developing a theological model for deconstructing racialization and dismantling racism within contemporary American evangelical theology and practice. Racialization is a worldview that, in spite of biological evidence to the contrary, organizes humans into racial groupings purportedly based on biology – rendering some racial groups inferior to others. In this book, I argue that the racism that still exists today within contemporary evangelicalism is a by-product of a racialized worldview. Moreover, I argue that although the efforts of major nineteenth and twentieth century black thinkers and theologians – such as Booker T. Washington, W.E.B. DuBois, James Cone, Gayraud Wilmore, and J. Deotis Roberts – have managed to establish the ground for racial integration, their work has not adequately addressed the root problem of racialization. In conversation with these thinkers and theologians, I argue that John M. Perkins' work provides a theological and practical framework that not only addresses the problem of racism, but also deconstructs racialization and works towards reconciliation and community development among a range of cultural and ethnic groups within the evangelical church.

# INTRODUCTION

In 1958, Martin Luther King observed that eleven o'clock Sunday morning is the most segregated hour of the week. In 1993, Billy Graham claimed racism to be one of the greatest deterrents to world evangelism.[1] More recently, Michael Emerson and Christian Smith's widely quoted sociological study, *Divided by Faith: Evangelical Religion and the Problem of Race in America*, attests to the fact that racism remains a central problem within American evangelical churches.[2] Their findings are corroborated by other major studies of race and religion – including Ronald H. Bayer's *The Columbia Documentary History of Race and Ethnicity in America*, Eric Lincoln's *Race, Religion, and the Continuing American Dilemma*, and John Bartkoski and Helen Regis's *Charitable Choices: Religion, Race, and Poverty in the Post-Welfare Era*.[3] It is also corroborated by personal testimony, as in Edward Gilbreath's *Reconciliation Blues: A Black Evangelical's Inside View of White Christianity*.[4]

1 Billy Graham, "Racism and the Evangelical Church," Christianity Today, 4 October 1993, 27.

2 Michael O. Emerson and Christian Smith, Divided by Faith: Evangelical Religion and the Problem of Race in America (New York: Oxford University Press, 2001), 11.

3 See C. Eric Lincoln, Race, Religion, and the Continuing American Dilemma (New York: Hill and Wang, 1999); Ronald H. Bayor, The Columbia Documentary History of Race and Ethnicity in America (New York: Columbia University Press, 2004); and John Bartkoski and Helen Regis. Charitable Choices: Religion, Race, and Poverty in the Post-Welfare Era (New York: New York University Press, 2003).

4 Edward Gilbreath, *Reconciliation Blues: A Black Evangelical's Inside View of White Christianity* (Downers Grove, IL: InterVarsity Books, 2008).

To cite further examples, *The Journal of Blacks in Higher Education* presents statistics suggesting that member colleges in the Counsel of Christian Colleges and Universities (CCCU) are far from racial parity,[5] as does another recent study of evangelical colleges.[6] Northwestern College, in St. Paul Minnesota, is a typical example of a CCCU School that has made intentional efforts to address these issues. However, the efforts have resulted in less than parity with 3 percent black student population and less than 3.5 percent full-time faculty. In an unpublished survey of graduating seniors completed in 2008 at Northwestern College, 66.9 percent cited racial tension and 31.6 percent cited hearing faculty express stereotypes about racial and ethnic groups.[7]

An evangelical denomination, the Evangelical Free Church in America, provides yet another example of a failure to move toward racial parity within the evangelical church. In the late 1980s, the first African American was ordained in the Evangelical Free Church of America. Most of the first wave of 16 African American senior pastors in place by 1990 left the church within three years, frustrated and disillusioned with the lack of progress made by the denomination. In 2004, 2006, and 2008 three new minorities, two African American and one Hispanic, were hired by the Evangelical Free Church to give leadership in the area of diversity. Given the demographics that the United States population is represented by at least 33 percent minority and 12.5 percent African American, parity has not been reached in, at least, this denomination.[8]

---

5 "Black Enrollments at Christian Colleges Are on the Rise," The Journal of Blacks in Higher Education (August 7, 2008), http://www.jbhe.com (accessed January 13, 2009).

6 A. B. Caneday, "In the Name of the Father, the Son, and the Spirit of Diversity: Multiculturalism Goes to College," Christian Research Institute 3, no. 2 (2007).

7 Northwestern College, 2008.

8 Pew Research Center, "US Population Projections 2005-2050," under Social and Demographic Trends, Jeffrey S. Passel and D'Vera Cohn (February 11, 2008), http://www.docstoc.com/ (accessed January 13, 2009).

In this study, I use the concept of racialization as a means for addressing the problem of racism in the evangelical church. Racialization is a worldview that – in spite of biological evidence to the contrary – socially constructs differences among human beings based on racial groupings purportedly based on biology. Ashley Montagu first introduced the concept in *Man's Most Dangerous Myth: The Fallacy of Race* (1942), which was published after the atrocities of Hitler in World War II. In his introduction to the sixth edition (published in 1997), Montagu succinctly states that the very concept of race is socially constructed and not based on biologically determined factors:

> The purpose of the present, sixth edition is to make use of the scientifically established facts to show that the term "race" is a socially constructed artifact – that there is no such thing in reality as "race"; that the very word is racist; that the idea of "race," implying the existence of significant biologically determined mental differences rendering some populations inferior to others, is wholly false; and that the space between an idea and reality can be very great and misleading.[9]

The transcript of the PBS documentary *Race, The Power of an Illusion* (2003) provides a significant list of biologists and geneticists who support Montagu's position.[10]

Theological and philosophical criticisms of the use of a "racial matrix" for distinguishing among human beings can be found in Cornel West's *Race Matters*, which links it to "White racism,"[11] and Victor Anderson's *Beyond Ontological Blackness*, which offers a critique of any attempt to create an "ontology" based on

---

9 Ashley Montagu, *Man's Most Dangerous Myth: The Fallacy of Race*, 6th ed. (Walnut Creek, CA: AltaMira, 1997), 31.

10 California Newsreel, *Race: The Power of an Illusion*, DVD transcript, executive producer Larry Adelman, 2003, *http://www.*newsreel.org/transcripts/race2.htm (accessed August 8, 2008).

11 Cornel West, *Race Matters* (New York: Vintage Books, 1993), 39.

the distinction between "Whiteness" and "Blackness."[12] In addition, an important historical critique of the social construction of the concept of race is Thomas F. Gossett's *Race: The History of an Idea in America.*[13]

In this book, I examine some of the major thinkers who have influenced the development of black theology in America and argue that although they made significant contributions to the fight against racism, they did not adequately deal with the underlying problem of racialization. Although Booker T. Washington (1854-1915), for example, offered important early solutions to the problem of race relations in the United States, he chose to address the issue, almost exclusively, from an economic point of view rather than from theological and anthropological points of view.[14] Furthermore, even his pleas for economic equity in his famous *Atlanta Compromise* speech had little effect on the social structure of American life. The next year, 1896, the Supreme Court of the United States handed down a decision upholding the policy of "separate but equal" in the landmark case of Plessy versus Ferguson, a decision that had a profound effect on American racial relations, including racial relations within the church.

W.E.B. DuBois' life and work (1868-1963) overlapped Washington's and lasted well into the twentieth century.[15] He challenged Washington's position of compromise and instead took the stance of an agitator. One of his greatest contributions, the establishment of the National Association for the Advancement of Colored People (NAACP), has been agitating and fighting against racism for 100 years – laying the ground for a legal battle against racism and establishing a generation of social integration policies,

12 Victor Anderson, *Beyond Ontological Blackness: An Essay on African American Religious and Cultural Criticism* (New York: Continuum, 1995), 117.

13 Thomas F. Gossett, *Race: The History of an Idea in America* (New York: Oxford Press, 1997).

14 See the bibliography for a list of his works.

15 See the bibliography for a list of his works.

which have lasted into the twenty-first century. DuBois rejected the work of the race theorists who were suggesting from four to dozens of races, reportedly supported by biology and genetics, because he was well aware of the research that discredited their conclusions. However, despite his knowledge of the discredited theories about race, DuBois chose to ignore the battle against racialization because, in his mind, eliminating racial categories would result in the assimilation of black people by the white majority. In his view, even if the American melting pot managed to develop a shared understanding of citizenship – and a shared language, religion, and set of political ideals – it could not create an identity that was inclusive enough to overcome the distinctions created by racialization.

Nonetheless, DuBois established the intellectual ground for the later black theology movement led by James Cone, Gayraud Wilmore, and J. Deotis Roberts.[16] These theologians chose to focus the attention of "black theology" on a critique of racism in "white theology" – with Cone offering a theological critique, with Wilmore offering a historic critique, and with Roberts offering a philosophical critique.[17]

Cone argued that white theology focuses on theological concepts and questions relevant to another era – such as the period of the Church Councils of Nicea and Chalcedon. The Jesus of Luther, Calvin and Barth, therefore, is a Jesus based on these theological concepts. By contrast, Cone contends that the Jesus that he relates to – and the Jesus black people have related to from the beginning – is a Jesus who is present with them in the midst of their suffering and experiences of oppression. White theology is racist, he argues, because it is written from a white point of view and does not consider the experiences of black people. For theology to be truly representative of the gospel of Jesus Christ to black people, it must be black theology; black

16 See the bibliography of a list of works by Cone, Wilmore, and Roberts.
17 See, e.g., Cone's work for the use of these terms.

theology must articulate a theology that interprets the biblical text and the gospel from the standpoint of black people's experiences. The positive implication of Cone's argument is that it lends dignity to people whose experience has been overlooked when it comes to doing theology – by creating space at the table for their voices. The negative implication of his view, however, is that Cone's point of view demonstrates how black theology's emphasis on race makes it difficult to offer solutions to the problems of racialization and ethnocentrism – and by implication, racism as well – because black theology continues to work within the matrix created by a racialized worldview. Any solution offered by black theology is still limited by this worldview.

Unlike Cone, Wilmore does make overtures toward addressing racialization, but because he insists on maintaining racial identity as a significant source of self-esteem, a racialized worldview remains at the center of his work. Wilmore served as a pastor and a theologian, but his greatest contributions came in his role as a church historian. He documented the history of black religion and served on several black church councils during and after the civil rights movement of the 1950s, 1960s, and 1970s. Wilmore addressed racialization in church society, insisting that "racial identity should be no bar to full fellowship and participation in the church and in society,"[18] and believing that an integrated society and church is possible. However, in order for this integration to take place, white Christians need to acquire an appreciation for the particular experience of black humanity in American life. This experience has created a sensibility and perception rarely identical with those born white in America. For Wilmore, integration needs to proceed beyond the superficial, which means that blacks and other people of color need to be empowered

18 Gayraud S. Wilmore and James H. Cone, eds., *Black Theology: A Documentary History, 1966-1979* (Maryknoll, NY: Orbis Books, 1979), 95.

to have a healthy sense of their own racial identity as a subculture within the larger white culture.

Roberts differs from Cone and Wilmore in that he explicitly identifies himself as an evangelical, who espouses a conservative view of the Bible's authority.[19] His most important contribution is his theological and philosophical critique of white evangelical theology. In his work, he brings to the fore several observations about their theology that most whites overlook. First, Roberts argues that much of white theology is influenced by a European worldview, which, in turn, is heavily influenced by Greek philosophical premises. Influenced by Aristotle and Plato, this worldview assumes that it represents the totality of human philosophical thought. However, this position puts white theologians at a decided disadvantage. Although their cultural context is European and Greek, many white Christians believe that they represent cultural neutrality. Roberts argues that this position is arrogant; rather, he argues, "it is more honest to admit our particularities."[20] Although he recognizes the need for a "universal understanding," say for interpreting biblical texts – presupposing that the Bible is, indeed, the Word of God for all people – he nonetheless contends that we need to have a multicultural approach in our attempts at interpreting the Bible. Roberts suggests that the lack of multicultural input produces an ethic driven by an ethnocentric ideology rather than biblical theology. The lack of multicultural input – and the ethnocentric perspective it presupposes – perpetuates racism in ways difficult for white people to recognize.

My analysis of the efforts of these black thinkers – from the early period (Washington and DuBois), on to the flowering of black theology (Cone and Wilmore) and the case for an evangelical black

19 See the bibliography for a list of his work.

20 J. Deotis Roberts, "Contextual Theology: Liberation and Indigenization," *ChickenBones: A Journal for Literary and Artistic African American Themes,* http://nathanielturner.com/contextualtheology.htm (accessed August 24, 2008). Also available in print version: *The Christian Century* (January 28, 1976).

theology (with Roberts) – lays the groundwork for my analysis of Perkins' contributions. Although I will draw on each of their contributions to black theology and their important contributions to the critique of racism in white theology, I will nonetheless make the case that each of them – albeit in different ways – does not adequately deal with the problem of racialization. In spite of the significant ground-breaking contributions of Washington and DuBois and the insights into the racism embedded in white theology offered by Cone, Wilmore and Roberts, the problem of racialization must be addressed more fully.

In order to address this problem, I will examine John Perkins' practical theology rooted in community development work, in order to lay the groundwork for developing a framework not only for dismantling racism, but also for deconstructing racialization and seeking reconciliation among diverse ethnic and cultural groups within the evangelical church. I will analyze how his emphasis on our identity "in Christ" (which transcends our attempts to establish "compensatory identities," racial or otherwise) and his model for "depersonalizing racism" (which seeks to deconstruct our socio-political constructs of whiteness and blackness) subvert the myth of race and strip racialization of its power.[21]

I will argue that Perkins' approach to addressing the problem of racism has two central biblical premises, premises at the core of his identity as an evangelical Christian: our being created in the "image of God" (Gen 1:28) and our identity "in Christ," as those who have received, by faith in Jesus Christ, an identity of "sonship" (Gal 4:6; Rom 8:15). When we lose our sense of being created in God's image, we fill the void with identities that compensate for the loss of our real identity, such as those identified with racial typological categories – for example, Negroid, Caucasoid, and Mongoloid, among many

21 See the bibliography for a list of his work.

others. When we presuppose these compensatory identities as our fundamental identity, we limit the progress that can be made in reducing the effects of racialization because the players are always caught in a "them and us matrix" – a matrix that maintains the competition noted by Shelby Steele, where the races are constantly "fighting for innocence."[22] In support of these insights, I should note that Cornel West also recognizes the futility of the racial matrix, noting its relationship to white racism.[23] In addition, Victor Anderson's ground-breaking work on "ontological Blackness" provides a philosophical analysis of the difficulties inherent in a racial matrix.[24]

Presupposing our being created in God's image and our identity in Christ, Perkins seeks to "depersonalize racism" by treating it as a manifestation of the sin that affects "real people" – an insight he arrived at in an epiphany while in jail.[25] By treating racism as sin, Perkins allows racism to be objectified and capable of being dealt with by all members of the Christian community. Guilt for racism can then be understood objectively and assessed in terms of the interplay between real people. Culpability, then, for individuals, can be assessed to those who have earned guilt. In an atmosphere of depersonalized racism, the work of building community has the potential of going forward without its racially and culturally diverse membership attacking each other. It has the potential for dealing with racism with repentance, forgiveness, and reconciliation.

Perkins' model allows for the development of a truly reconciled, multiracial, multi-ethnic, and multicultural Christian community. It allows us to view one another as real people and not simply from the

---

22 Shelby Steele, *The Content of Our Character: A New Vision of Race in America* (New York: Harper Collins, 1991), 11.
23 West, *Race Matters*, 39.
24 Victor Anderson, *Beyond Ontological Blackness: An Assay on African American Religious and Cultural Criticism* (New York: Continuum, 1995), 117.
25 Stephen Berk, *A Time to Heal* (Grand Rapids: Baker Books, 1997).

standpoint of supposedly inherent distinctions based on the social constructs of whiteness and blackness. Perkins' biblical model not only addresses the problem of racism by depersonalizing it, but it also positions the church to address ethnocentrism in its attempt at community development. By draining racialization of power, Perkins' model is able to embrace the balance taught by the apostle Paul of validating ethnic and cultural distinctiveness, while offering spiritual maturity as the solution for the sins that are ethnocentric in emphasis. Models based on inherent distinctions between black theology and white theology are still trapped within the racial matrix and cannot offer this kind of balance. They are, in fact, ethnocentric in nature themselves. By contrast, John Perkins' biblically based evangelical theology offers the identity category of "sonship" (or being "in Christ") as a way out of the racial matrix. As such, his Christ-centered, spiritually based model stands as a new paradigm for building Christian community in contrast to old paradigms based on a racialized worldview.

In sum, I address a twofold problem in this study. On the one hand, I argue that because much evangelical theology and practice remains racialized, it also remains racist in many of its practices. Thus, its doctrines of creation and salvation in Christ have done little to move evangelicals toward reconciliation. On the other hand, I argue that although black theology and black theologians have brought to the fore the problem of racism in Christian theology, they do not adequately address the critical problem of racialization.

In order to address the evangelical church's continued problem of racism and racialization, I will first offer a short history of racialization. This will provide the background for a critical analysis of the development of black theology in America within the work of its seminal figures. My discussion will begin with the early contributions of Washington and DuBois, which resulted in surface levels of integration and racial equity and initially laid the framework for addressing racism in American theology and culture. I will then assess the later contributions by Cone, Wilmore, and Roberts as they developed a much more incisive critique of racism in white theology. I will argue that although these theologians have offered important critiques of the racism embedded in white theology and culture, they still have not addressed the problem of racialization, since they continue to work within the matrix of racialized assumptions about human variation. Although the work of these theologians has the potential for helping evangelicals to consider racial equity on a denominational level and integration in local church congregations, they still do not address the underlying sources of racism generated by a racialized worldview.

I will offer an interpretation of Perkins' practical theology of community development and argue that it proposes a means for addressing racism by way of a theology that moves beyond racialization. In making this case, I bring to the fore two major assumptions inherent in his biblically based evangelical theology and demonstrate their import for his treatment of the problem of racism and racialization. First, we are created in God's image (Gen 1:28) and, second, we are adopted by faith in Jesus Christ into a new relationship of "sonship" with the Father through the Spirit (Gal 4:6; Rom 8:15). These two premises provide a response to our creation of compensatory racial identities, classically identified with the fall (Gen 3). These premises ground Perkins' model for dealing with race relations in ways that move beyond racialization and lay the foundation for his work toward racial reconciliation and a Christian approach to community development.

# CHAPTER ONE

*A Short History of Racialization*

John Perkins' understanding that our identity in Christ must be experienced as our primary identity addresses the historic problem of *racialization* in the church.[26] This position effectively reconfigures the distortions presented by a racialized worldview. Racialization is a worldview with roots in Aristotelian politics. It is a worldview that has had a profound influence throughout the history of western culture. It is a worldview responsible for much of the systemic and individual racism still holding the world in bondage. It heavily influences the praxis of medical science, social science, and theology with its greatest damage being done after the Age of Enlightenment.

## METHODOLOGY

Ivan Hannaford in his work *Race: The History of an Idea in the West* and Cornel West in his work *Prophesy Deliverance* suggest the development of a racialized worldview began in the area of methodology:

26 Racialization is a worldview that, in spite of biological evidence to the contrary, organizes humans into racial groupings purportedly based on biology – rendering some racial groups inferior to others. See Preface, 5.

> The first stage involves three complicated changes. The first and most important has to do with methodology – the setting of the metaphysical and theological scheme of things for a more logical description and classification that ordered humankind in terms of physiological and mental criteria based on observable "facts" and tested evidence.[27]

Methodology was developed around the ability to organize human beings into observable and testable categories based on physical traits. West, in agreement with Hannaford, takes the observations a bit further by posing implicit racist implications:

> The creative fusion of scientific investigation, Cartesian epistemology, and classical ideals produced forms of rationality, scientificity, and objectivity which, though efficacious in the quest for truth and knowledge, prohibited the intelligibility and legitimacy of the ideas of black equality in beauty, culture, and intellectual capacity. In fact, to "think" such an idea was to be deemed irrational, barbaric, or mad.[28]

According to Cornel West, the Greek ideal forms provided the standard for beauty, and the scientific revolution, coupled with Cartesians philosophy, provided the system to measure and compare. These ideas were adopted and adapted by eighteenth, nineteenth, and twentieth century thinkers and became perfect building blocks for racialization leading to individual and systemic racism. Both men agree that the foundation feeding into a racialized worldview was to be found in Aristotle's *The Politics*. Aristotle's discussion on slavery introduces the notion that certain men are born to be ruled while others were born to rule:

---

27 Ivan Hannaford, *Race: The History of an Idea in the West* (Baltimore: Johns Hopkins University Press, 1996), 187.

28 Cornel West, *Prophesy Deliverance: An Afro-American Revolutionary Christianity* (Louisville, KY: Westminster John Knox Press, 1982), 48.

> Ruling and being ruled belong not only among things necessary but also among things advantageous. And immediately from birth certain things diverge, some toward being ruled, others toward ruling. There are many kinds both of ruling and ruled [things], and the better rule is always that over ruled [things] that are better, for example over a human being rather than a beast; for the work performed by the better is better, and wherever something rules and something is ruled there is a certain work belonging to these together.[29]

In this view, bondage or freedom is part of a man's nature. The proper function of an individual is determined by birth. Therefore, living consistently with the nature of one's birth is advantageous to the state and the people involved. Aristotle goes on to say that all animals, as well as women, are inferior to man and by nature should be ruled by men because nature has made them for that purpose:

> The same holds with respect to man and the other animals: tame animals have a better nature than wild ones, and it is better for all of them to be ruled by man, since in this way their preservation is ensured. Further, the relation of male to female is by nature a relation of superior to inferior and ruler to ruled. The same must of necessity hold in the case of human beings generally. (8) Accordingly, those who are as different [from other men] as the soul from the body or man from beast – and they are in this state if their work is the use of the body, and if this is the best that can come from them – are slaves by nature. For them it is better to be ruled in accordance with this sort of rule, if such is the case for the other things mentioned. (9) For he is a slave by nature who is capable of belonging to another – which is also why he belongs to another – and who participates in reason only to the extent of perceiving it, but does not have it. (The other animals, not perceiving reason, obey their passions.) Moreover, the need for them differs only slightly: bodily

29 Aristotle, *The Politics*, trans. Carnes Lord (Chicago: The University of Chicago Press, 1984), 40.

> assistance in the necessary things is forthcoming from both, from slaves and from tame animals alike...[30]

Aristotle does not stop with his comparison of women and animals. He also extends his comparisons to human who have bodies, which are by nature, better for labor. They should be ruled by those who have minds to rule. Some of these lower level human beings, like animals, cannot reason. They can only perceive of reasoning. So, the notion of superior and inferior human being did not start in colonial American but at least as far back as the Ancient Greek philosophers.

## EXPLANATION

Studies of the history of racialization in the West and in the United States suggest that Europeans were attempting to explain the existence of humans with a variety of phenotypes. It was not until the late seventeenth century that the European scientists began serious work in the area of race theory. Francois Bernier was likely the first to publish on the subject of human differences in 1684. According to Thomas F. Gossett, the best scientific minds were focused on the sciences of physics and chemistry, the laws of motion and the effects of gravity. Work in the area of race theory was in its infancy. The assumption was that the creator decided what humans were like as evidence of his Glory:

> so scientific thought in the seventeenth and eighteenth centuries usually assumed that the Creator must personally have attended to the fabrication of every animal and plant on earth. An organism was what it was because God had decided it should be so. Its similarities with other organisms were

30 Ibid., 40-41.

> evidence of God's glory but in themselves were incidental and unimportant.[31]

With Bernier, as with others who made early attempts at human classification, the goal was to understand the general differences in appearance, not to justify social structure or to create a social stratification system. Most attempts at racial typology, with an end towards social stratification, were challenged by Enlightenment thinking because attributing character and intelligence to biology stood in juxtaposition to the theory of *tabula rasa*:

> Even if the situation in the biological sciences had been different, the temper of the eighteenth century would have found it difficult to assimilate theories of race superiority and inferiority. The emphasis upon universal reason was then enough to keep the philosophers of the Enlightenment uncomfortable in the presence of theories which implied conceptions of innate character and intelligence. It was the hope and belief of the Enlightenment that at birth the mind of a child is a tabula rasa, an empty receptacle. Education and environment could make this child into a completely reasonable and intelligent being. The idea that character is innate belonged, in this view, to discredited Calvinist ideas of predestination. If the mind of man should prove not to be a tabula rasa at the time of birth, then hopes for universal progress would receive a crushing blow. Thus race theories were considered a challenge to the optimism of the Enlightenment.[32]

In 1737, Leibnitz objected even to the mild classification suggested by Bernier. Leibnitz believed that even if there are differences of appearance and disposition among people from different parts of the earth "these differences are not enough to make Leibnitz accept the

---

31 Thomas F. Gossett, *Race: The History of an Idea in America* (New York: Oxford University Press, 1997), 33-34.

32 Ibid., 34.

idea of separate races. 'That … is no reason,' he says, 'why all men who inhabit the earth should not be of the same race.'"[33]

Carl Linnaeus, called the Father of Taxonomy, is credited for dividing mankind into four varieties: *Homo Europaeus, Homo Asiaticus, Homo Afer,* and *Homo Americanus.*[34] But he came short of suggesting different species of men. George Buffon and John Hunter each published works in the late eighteenth century discussing the differences in the race classification, but neither suggested the idea that the variety in humanity represented different species. They both suggested one race, with climate the responsible agent causing differences in appearance. However, one important observation in the work of these eighteenth century scientists is that they all believed that white was the norm and climate somehow made some people permanently darker.

In 1775, Johann Friedrich Blumenback published his dissertation *On the Natural Variety of Mankind.* Blumenback, known as the father of craniology and anthropology, suggested the well-known typological categories: Caucasian, Mongolian, Ethiopian, American, and Malay. Over his lifetime, Blumenback did extensive work on skull sizes and shapes. Blumenback's position on the superiority of races is disputed. Gossett and Montagu say that Blumenback did not conclude the superiority of any particular race based on biology. However, Cornel West, referencing George L. Mosse's, *Toward the Final Solution: A History of European Racism,* challenges their positions:

> Blumenback praised the symmetrical face as the most beautiful of human faces precisely because it approximated the "divine" works of Greek art, and specifically the proper anatomical proportions found in Greek sculpture. Applying

33 Ibid., 34-35.
34 Ibid., 35.

> the classical ideal of moderation, he claimed that the more moderate the climate, the more beautiful the face. The net result was that since black people were farthest from the Greek ideal and located in extremely hot climates, they were, by implication, inferior in beauty to Europeans.[35]

Whether Blumenback believed one race to be superior over another is probably not that important. That fact that he agreed with the suggestions of his day, that the character of an individual could be inherited and that the white race was the standard race, implying that darkness was some sort of aberration, went a long way to corroborate superiority theories developed in the nineteenth century. Others of the late eighteenth century continued to publish works supporting the notion that *race differences were caused by climate and that Negroes were innately the same as whites.*[36] Samuel Smith in 1787 and John Maclean in 1795 are among these scientists.

### *Thomas Jefferson's* ***Notes***

The researchers of the documentary *Race: the Power of an Illusion,* produced by California Newsreel in 2003, make the suggestion that Thomas Jefferson's comments published in his *Notes on Virginia* suggesting that *the Negro is condemned by nature to an inferior status* are among the first to take this position.

> PAUL FINKELMAN,[37] HISTORIAN: It is possible to make the argument that Thomas Jefferson is the first person to truly articulate a theory of race in the United States, and

35 Cornel West, *Prophesy Deliverance*, 57.

36 Gossett, *Race*, 39.

37 Paul Finkelman is President William McKinley Distinguished Professor of Law and Public Policy at Albany Law School. He is the author of many articles and books, including *Slavery and the Founders: Race and Liberty in the Age of Jefferson* (2001) and *A March of Liberty: A Constitutional History of the United States* (2002), and coeditor (with Martin J. Hershock) of *The History of Michigan Law* (2006).

> in effect, he has to do so. He has said in the Declaration of Independence, that we are all created equal. Well, if in fact we're all created equal, and if in fact we're entitled to our liberty, then how can he possibly own 175 slaves, and going up to about 225 slaves at the peak of his slave holding?
>
> NARRATOR: In Notes Jefferson's words appeared to justify slavery at a time when many slaves were admonishing the founding fathers for espousing freedom while continuing to support a system of human bondage.[38]

Jefferson goes to great length in his writing to demonstrate that the Negro's inferior status is not a result of *lack of opportunity* but a by-product of their nature.[39] Jefferson was very aware that his ideas flew in the face of the thinking during the Enlightenment. To suggest blacks to be a different race of men from whites would have been considered blasphemy and associated with atheism. Yet Jefferson came close to concluding whites and blacks to be distinct races[40]and therefore distinct species.

> Jefferson had read Buffon and was perhaps uneasily aware that his own opinion of Negroes was not shared by most of the men of his time who were specialists in natural history. We cannot "degrade a whole race of men from the work in the scale of beings which their creator may perhaps have given them," he says. "I advance it, therefore, as a suspicion only, that the blacks, whether originally a distinct race, or made distinct by time and circumstance, are inferior to the whites in the endowment both of body and of mind." At this point, Jefferson was very near a much more explosive issue than

38 California Newsreel, "The Story We Tell," episode 2 of *Race: The Power of an Illusion*, DVD, executive producer Larry Adelman, 2003, http://www.newsreel.org/transcripts/race2.htm (accessed August 8, 2008).
It is interesting to compare Jefferson's comments to the comment of Aristotle in his *Politics*. Jefferson's understanding of the word "race" in his time meant "different species."

39 Gossett, *Race*, 43-44.

40 California Newsreel, "The Story We Tell."

> the question of Negro equality. The idea that the Negroes might be a "distinct race" was then associated with atheism and blasphemy.[41]

Jefferson was among those who were taking a new position on race relations. This new position called the polygenist theory taught that blacks and whites had different origins. Among the supporters of the new polygenist theory were Voltaire in France, Lord Kames in Scotland, and Charles White in England.

> By the nineteenth century, defending slavery became an important issue in the West: The idea that Negroes are a separate species was still a curiosity in the eighteenth century, though the arguments of Voltaire, those of Kames, and especially those of White were to be repeated ad nauseam in nineteenth-century defenses of slavery. The great handicap which the theory of separate origin encountered was the fact that it cast doubt upon the biblical narrative, or at least required a rather special interpretation of it. In spite of his attempts to make the theory of separate origin of races square with scripture...[42]

## SUPERIORITY MAINTAINED

By the beginning of the nineteenth century, the die was cast. The Western worldview concerning the nature of the races was set. The theories varied from the notion that blacks and whites represented different species to their representing the same species, from monogenist to polygenist. The explanation for the variety of colors varied from climate and geography, to carbon being trapped in black skin, to blackness being a disease. Although theories of race varied

41 Gossett, *Race*, 43-44.
42 Ibid., 51.

a bit, one thing remained the same: White people were considered superior to black people and other people of color. The abolition of slavery did nothing to change this consistent opinion.

Darwin added a slightly new twist to the basic idea that blacks and other people of color were inferior to whites. Darwin changed the basis of race theory, but he did not change the argument that some races are superior to others.[43] There is, however, one significant change that Darwin's theory did bring to the study of race theory:

> The theory of evolution stimulated a movement which was already the chief interest of many nineteenth-century anthropologists – the measurement of race differences. If the races represented different stages of evolution, then it was important to measure their differences. These measurements might well indicate the direction in which evolution had proceeded. Only when the norms of the different races had been established could students of race speak of their field with something like the confidence with which biologists described species and varieties among the lower members of the natural world. Ambitious schemes for the measurement of race differences multiplied. The nineteenth century was a period of exhaustive and – as it turned out – futile search for criteria to define and describe race differences.[44]

In the middle of the nineteenth century, race anthropology turned toward the arduous task of defining and describing race differences. Not much has changed since the nineteenth century. Much of what is going on in medical research today assumes the validity of biological

43 Ibid., 67.
44 Ibid., 68-69.

race taxons. Robert Wallace,[45] quoting an op-ed by Armand Marie Leroi, says:

> Armand Marie Leroi announces in his Times op-ed that race is biologically real (*New York Times*, March 14, 2005). The crusty trope that race is a social artifact crumbles in the face of the bright new genomics, he asserts. Genetic variation may be greater within groups than between groups, as Richard Lewontin pointed out back in the dark ages of the 1970s, but only for single genes. Taken together, across genetic loci allelic distributions correlate into clusters long recognized as the five races: European, East Asian, African, Amerindian, and Australasian. So suck it up, constructionists, race is biologically intrinsic. [46]

Wallace responded to Leroi's *Time* article saying:

> Leroi and the new racialists are trying to get around population thinking by correlating aggregations across loci, as a set of emergent essentialisms. Funny, though, that within the very medical framework they are attempting to define, as they live by the sword of correlation, so must they die by that sword. When we correlate putative racial continua across diseases, the same groups are time and again imputed the most susceptible alleles. African Americans suffer not only greater prevalence of and/or lesser survivorship from heart disease (Andrews et al. 2001) and prostate cancer (Reddy et al. 2003), as Leroi notes, but thc samc for kidncy cancer (Vaishampayan et al. 2003), breast cancer (Ghafoor et al. 2003), cervical cancer (Jemal et al. 2004), oral cancers (Shavers et al. 2003), lung cancer (Stellman et al. 2003),

45 Robert Wallace is a research associate in the Department of Biology at the City College of New York. Dr. Wallace's current work focuses on the evolutionary ecology of HIV and Kaposi's sarcoma-associated herpes virus. He quotes from an article entitled "A Racialized Medical Genomics: Bright and Wrong" for the California Newsreel documentary *Race: The Power of An Illusion*, in addition to the *New York Times* op-ed article.

46 Robert Wallace, "A Racialized Medical Genomics: Shiny, Bright and Wrong," in *Race: The Power of an Illusion*, "Background Readings," *PBS* (California Newsreel: 2003), http://www.pbs.org/race/000_About/002_04-background-01-13.htm (accessed August 11, 2008).

> colorectal cancer (Baguet and Commiskey 1999), pancreatic cancer (Silverman et al. 2003), endometrical cancer (Randall and Armstrong 2003), lymphomas (Briggs et al. 2003), tooth loss (Gilbert et al. 2003), obesity and diabetes (Cossrow and Faulkner 2004), chronic asthma (Boudreaux et al. 2003), Lupus nephritis (Lea 2002), HIV (Torian et al. 2002), hepatitis B and syphilis (Schrag et al. 2003), gonorrhea (Dombrowski et al. 2004), arthritis (Dunlop et al. 2001), stroke (Ruland and Gorelick 2005), and so on...Are we to assume that African Americans and other minority groups carry the most susceptible alleles for every one of these diseases? Can we pretend that the vagaries of mutational chance just happened to deal African Americans the greatest susceptibilities for every ailment on our awful list? While there are indeed well-documented examples of illness with important genetic roots, for a framework addressing health disparities we'd exert greater impact by placing our attention back on the man behind the curtain. Racism and other sources of population-level stress have, by way of their emotional and material deprivations, definitional effect on individuals as early as conception, as well as on the populations of which they are a part. Racism shapes ontogeny, regardless of allelic frequencies. And it's to that relationship and its overdetermination of the correlation of diseases where research and social action need to be directed.[47]

If Wallace is correct in his critique of Leroi's position, then two very important conclusions can be drawn. First, the effects of racism are supporting the continued illusion of racial typology. Secondly, racialization and racism are heavily influencing the medical profession and the health of African Americans and other people of color.

Ritchie Witzig[48] confirms Wallace's comments:

47 Ibid.

48 Ritchie Witzig, Infectious Diseases Physician and Assistant Professor of Tropical Medicine at the Tulane School of Public Health, New Orleans, Louisiana.

> Changing the social identifiers of patients from a few unscientific race taxons to a larger and more diverse set of ethnic designations may be more meaningful, but it would probably be unpopular with bureaucrats and researchers. Although race groupings are not biologically or anthropologically relevant, some may argue 1) that they should stay intact for the sake of continuity and 2) that ethnic identification is unnecessary and is simply done to achieve political correctness. Evidence from scientific and ethical viewpoints shows that this view is incorrect and that medical interpretation of race fortify popular societal usage. The athlete and scholar Arthur Ashe once contrasted the effect on his life of his ethnicity with that of the acquired immunodeficiency syndrome (AIDS), of which he died. Many were surprised by his statement that "being black is the greatest burden ... a more onerous burden than AIDS." Institutional racism is common in society and medicine in the United States; arbitrary race grouping is part of such racism. Studies have documented that medical rationing based on ethnicity occurs in the United States and have detailed the ethnic bias that affects the treatment plans of some physicians. Such biases are inexcusable in medicine. Our moral responsibility as health professionals is to invest a physical and mental orientation in each patient that is optimal for maintaining and recovering health. This imperative includes empowering patients to define themselves (and their ethnicities) rather than labeling them according to a social construct that masquerades as scientific fact. At best, such labeling results in alienation; at worst, it causes medical mismanagement.[49]

Witzig suggests that, in some cases, American medical professionals are actually practicing racism by the way medical advice and resources are distributed.

---

49 Ritchie Witzig, "The Medicalization of Race: Scientific Legitimization of a Flawed Social Construct," *Annals of Internal Medicine* 125 (1996), http://annals.highwire.org/cgi/content/full/125/8/675 (accessed August 11, 2008).

## THE MYTH OF RACE

Shortly before the close of the Second World War, literature questioning the legitimacy of racial stratification based on biology began to be published. One of the first was by Ashley Montagu, in 1942, entitled *Man's Most Dangerous Myth: The Fallacy of Race*. In the 1972 edition Montagu says, "This book then is designed to expose the most dangerous myth of our age, the myth of 'race,' 'the formidable doctrine of Race' as Emerson had already called it more than a century ago, by demonstrating the falsities of which it is compounded."[50] He goes on to quote the Joint Commission on Mental Health in Children, published in 1970. It stated that racism is the number one public health problem facing Americans today.[51]

In 2003, PBS published a documentary entitled *Race – The Power of an Illusion* highlighting current research supporting the fact that racial stratification has no basis in biology but is, in fact, a sociopolitical construct. "There is not one gene, trait, or characteristic that distinguishes all members of one race from all members of another. We can map any number of traits and none would match our idea of race."[52]

The documentary published a statement from an interview with Alan Goodman, professor of biological anthropology at Hampshire College and co-editor of *Genetic Nature / Culture: Anthropology and Science Beyond the Cultural Divide and Building a New Bio-Cultural Synthesis*:

> To understand why the idea of race is a biological myth requires a major paradigm shift - an absolutely [sic] paradigm

50 Ashley Montagu, *Man's Most Dangerous Myth: The Fallacy of Race*, 5th ed. (London: Oxford University Press, 1974), x.

51 Ibid., xii.

52 PBS, *Race: The Power of an Illusion, PBS,* executive producer Larry Adelman (California Newsreel: 2003), http://www.pbs.org/race/000 About/002 04-background-01-11.htm (accessed July 27, 2008).

> shift, a shift in perspective. And for me, it's like seeing what it must have been like to understand that the world isn't flat. The world looks flat to our eyes. And perhaps I can invite you to a mountaintop or to a plain, and you can look out the window at the horizon, and see, "Oh, what I thought was flat I can see a curve in now." And that race is not based on biology, but race is rather an idea that we ascribe to biology… Scientists have actually been saying for quite a while that race, as biology, doesn't exist - that there's no biological basis for race. And that is in the facts of biology, the facts of non-concordance, the facts of continuous variation, the recentness of our evolution, the way that we all commingle and come together, how genes flow, and perhaps especially in the fact that most variation occurs within races versus between races or among races, suggesting that there's no generalizability to race. There is no center there; there is no there in the center. It's fluid.[53]

The documentary also published a short paper listing the findings of its research. The research not only validated the idea that race is a sociological construct with no support from biology but it also draws some important conclusions about the historic relationships between race and slavery and race and inequality:[54]

> Race is a powerful social idea that gives people different access to opportunities and resources. Our government and social institutions have created advantages that disproportionately channel wealth, power, and resources to white people. This affects everyone, whether we are aware of it or not.[55]

In the concluding paragraph from his 1998 Anthropology Newsletter article, Goodman makes the connection between the racialized worldview and systemic and individual racism.

53 PBS, *Race*.
54 For the entire list, see appendix: "Ten Things Everyone Should Know about Race."
55 PBS, *Race*.

Racialization, and what W.E.B. DuBois calls "Veil ideology," establishes the foundation for racism. If racism is going to be effectively addressed, the ideologies of the Veil must be deconstructed. Anything less will prove ineffective:

> Human biological variability is real. But race is a biological sham: it is theoretically passé, does not fit the facts, holds back science and causes harm. A common sleight of hand of the political right is to conflate the myth of biological race with the cultural experience of race, e.g., "If race is a (biological) myth, let's get rid of affirmative action." But the truth is just the opposite. Showing that race is a biological myth leads us to clarify the sociopolitical salience of race and racism. Race as biology does not explain the persistent and shameful rate at which black babies suffer low birth weight and infant mortality. It doesn't explain why the death rate from breast cancer recently fell for all women but did not budge for black women, who already had a higher rate of death. Nor does race as biology explain why black male life expectancy in Harlem is less than the life expectancy of men in Bangladesh. But the suffering is still there.[56]
>
> There is no half way between seeing race as biologically valid or not. Any reformation of race as biology will simply be interpreted as race in the older typological paradigm. What do we lose by giving up race as a biological concept? We lost some instant recognition of what we do. It takes a bit longer to explain human variation. What do we gain by sending race to the dust heap of history? The possibilities are awesome. We could develop a new and exciting biocultural paradigm. More important still, we would literally save lives.[57]

The conclusions drawn by Goodman and the team of researchers support, without qualification, the need to address the racialized elements of Western society.

---

56 Ibid.
57 Ibid.

## CHAPTER TWO

*Booker T. Washington and W.E.B. DuBois*

A study reviewing the history of black people and their struggle for social justice in American cannot overlook the contributions of Booker T. Washington and W.E.B. DuBois. Washington and DuBois had similar agendas to end systemic and individual racism prevalent in late nineteenth century and early twentieth century America. Each wanted an immediate end to the lynching of African Americans taking place at an epidemic pace all over the United States. Each wanted political, economic and social justice for all people and in particular people of color. The difference in their agendas becomes apparent in their strategies to reach their intended goals for justice. Washington sought to better the economic conditions of blacks; DuBois sought to address the deeper problem of racism in American society. Nonetheless, as I will argue, both men overlooked the centrality of racialization as a core issue fueling the race relations dynamics of the nineteenth and early twentieth centuries.

### WASHINGTON

A political leader, educator, and author, Washington (1854-1915) was the dominant figure in the American black community in the

United States from 1890 to 1915. Representing the last generation of black leaders born in slavery, his educational programs were supported not only by members of the black community, but also by powerful whites. He is best known for his skillful accommodation to the social realities of the age of segregation. His work flourished during the height of the white backlash in the South against Northern military occupation and African-American political success, as well as the destructive system of sharecropping. Because of these factors, Washington took a position of compromise and strove for the survival of black people rather than to challenge racialization. His focus was on establishing a basic economic foundation for black survival. Although the work for economic stability was important, and the establishment of Tuskegee Institute was a great accomplishment, his decision to compromise with whites became paradigmatic for his generation and the generation of black people that followed.

### *The Atlanta Compromise*

Washington authored four books during his lifetime – *The Story of My Life and Work (1900)*, *Up From Slavery* (1901), *My Larger Education* (1911), *The Man Farthest Down (1912)* – but he best known for a famous address, which came to be called "The Atlanta Compromise."[58] On September 18, 1895, African-American spokesman and leader Booker T. Washington spoke before a predominantly white audience at the Cotton States and International Exposition in Atlanta. His speech at this address is probably one of the most influential speeches in American history dealing with racial questions. Although the organizers of the conference were

58 Washington's complete works can be found in *The Booker T. Washington Papers*, ed. Louis R. Harlan, 14 vols. (Urban, IL: University of Illinois Press, 1972-1989), which can also be found at http://historymatters.gmu.edu. For a biography of Washington's life, see Robert J. Norrell, *Up from History: The Life of Booker T. Washington* (Cambridge: Belknap Press of Harvard University Press, 2009).

concerned that the larger white public was not ready for such a speech from a black speaker, they decided that inviting a black speaker would impress Northern visitors with the evidence of racial progress in the South. In his speech, Washington soothed his white listeners' concerns about blacks.

> As we have proved our loyalty to you in the past, in nursing your children, watching by the sick-bed of your mothers and fathers, and often following them with tear-dimmed eyes to their graves, so in the future, in our humble way, we shall stand by you with a devotion that no foreigner can approach, ready to lay down our lives, if need be, in defense of yours, interlacing our industrial, commercial, civil, and religious life with yours in a way that shall make the interests of both races one. In all things that are purely social we can be as separate as the fingers, yet one as the hand in all things essential to mutual progress.[59]

The speech revealed the agenda and strategy employed by Washington. In it, he articulated his understanding for the potential future relationship between blacks and whites. He also outlined a number of important concessions that he was willing to make. These strategies and concessions became the predominant doctrine sculpting the landscape for the American social structure for almost fifty years.

Washington began by giving the white man of the South positive strokes for making the initial effort to honor blacks, evidenced by their invitation to include blacks in their convention. The only black person included in the program was Washington himself. Washington believed that this invitation would do more to cement the friendship of the two races then any occurrence since the "dawn

59 See the "Atlanta Compromise Speech" in *The Booker T. Washington Papers*, Harlan, vol. 3, 583–587.

of our freedom."[60] Washington believed, or at least he communicated to the white audience that he believed, that the large number of blacks who were elected to congress during and right after the reconstruction was a mistake. If it was not a mistake, it was at least the wrong emphasis. It was the "ignorant and inexperienced" who focused on "political convention or stump speaking" rather than "starting a dairy farm or truck garden."[61]

Washington believed that blacks should "cast down your bucket where you are," meaning that blacks should start with what they have rather than insisting, through agitation, on immediate social, political, or economic equality. He understood blacks to be sitting on opportunities that had not been exercised. He believed that blacks should "begin at the bottom of life, and not the top."[62] Washington said, "Nor should we permit our grievances to overshadow our opportunities."[63] The question was whether Washington was willing to deal with the grievances or simply allow the status quo to be maintained. Later, DuBois believed that Washington was not willing to address the grievances at all. However, this is not the case. Washington believed that if the African- American population proved itself worth the respect of the white man, then the white man would give him that earned respect.

Washington's "Atlanta Compromise Speech" not only revealed his understanding of the relationship between blacks and whites, it also outlined a number of promises or concessions that blacks would make to whites. These promises outraged many blacks, but they also managed to ease the consciences and fears of many whites. In the

60 Ibid.
61 Ibid.
62 Ibid.
63 Ibid.

end, the concessions and strategies had only a limited success, but they did manage to serve at least part of the intended end.

Washington promised that the black man would have a greater devotion to the establishment than the new white immigrants coming from Europe would. He based his promises on the already earned trust of the white man and on past loyalty, "in nursing your children, watching by the sick-bed of your mothers and fathers and often following them with ear-dinned eyes to their graves."[64] In the future, Washington said, "we shall stand by you with a devotion that no foreigner can approach. We shall be ready to lay down our lives, if need be."[65] Washington promised that when it came to industrial and religious life, "We shall be interlacing our industrial, commercial, civil, and religious life with yours in a way that shall make the interests of both races one."[66]

Washington promised the white society that while they worked together, black and white, blacks would not expect to interact socially with whites but remain segregated. The social interaction would be limited to areas necessary for the mutual success of each race. Washington used an ingenious metaphor to communicate his intentions, "In all things that are purely social we can be as separate as the fingers, yet one as the hand in all things essential to mutual progress."[67]

Washington played to whites by attempting to diminish their fears. In doing so, he employed an interesting strategy. Each of the promises acted to guarantee that blacks would not challenge whites by working with them:

---

64 Ibid.
65 Ibid.
66 Ibid.
67 Ibid.

> Nearly sixteen millions of hands will aid you in pulling the load upward, or they will pull against you the load downward. We shall constitute one-third and more of the ignorance and crime of the South, or one-third [of] its intelligence and progress; we shall contribute one-third to the business and industrial prosperity of the South, or we shall prove a veritable body of death, stagnating, depressing, retarding every effort to advance the body politic.[68]

It appears that Washington's promises also revealed a veiled threat toward the white community. The threat came not with a promise of challenge from blacks but a prediction that if blacks were not included in the mainstream of American political and economic life, they would end up a drain on the political and economic life of white America. Making up one third of the population of the south, blacks were an important force to reckon with one way or another.

Although Washington never voiced his desire or his intention to strive for political and economic equity, he instead subtly communicated that these privileges were the ultimate goal at the end of the day. "No race that has anything to contribute to the markets of the world is long in any degree ostracized. It is important and right that all privileges of the law be ours, but it is vastly more important that we be prepared for the exercise of these privileges."[69]

Washington instead was willing to put himself and the entire black community in a position where they were dependent on the good will of whites to grant the privileges as the black community earned them.

> To those of the white race who look to the incoming of those of foreign birth and strange tongue and habits for the prosperity of the South, were I permitted I would repeat

68 Ibid.
69 Ibid.

> what I say to my own race, "Cast down your bucket where you are." Cast it down among the eight millions of Negroes whose habits you know, whose fidelity and love you have tested in days when to have proved treacherous meant the ruin of your firesides. Cast down your bucket among these people who have, without strikes and labor wars, tilled your fields, cleared your forests, built your railroads and cities, and brought forth treasures from the bowels of the earth, and helped make possible this magnificent representation of the progress of the South. Casting down your bucket among my people, helping and encouraging them as you are doing on these grounds, and to education of head, hand, and heart, you will find that they will buy your surplus land, make blossom the waste places in your fields, and run your factories. While doing this, you can be sure in the future, as in the past, that you and your families will be surrounded by the most patient, faithful, law-abiding, and unresentful people that the world has seen.[70]

Washington's strategy was to draw a picture that presented the black and white communities as mutually dependent on each other to build a prosperous community.

Washington built his argument on two important assumptions. First, given the opportunity and the right motivation, white people would do the right thing. Secondly, blacks had the ability, even under less-than-ideal circumstances (living as second-class citizens), to become productive citizens, willingly contributing to the prosperity of the white society. Instead of focusing his attention on social equality, Washington believed that the highest need for the black community was to earn a dollar, get an industrial education, and start their own businesses. Washington's position on this matter is clearly established in a personal commentary on his Atlanta Compromise speech. Writing in his book *Up From Slavery,* Washington says:

---

70 Ibid.

> In this address I said that the whole future of the Negro rested largely upon the question as to whether or not he should make himself, through his skill, intelligence, and character, of such undeniable value to the community in which he lived that the community could not dispense with his presence. I said that any individual who learned to do something better than anybody else – learned to do a common thing in an uncommon manner – had solved his problem, regardless of the colour of his skin, and that in proportion as the Negro learned to produce what other people wanted and must have, in the same proportion would he be respected.[71]

In Washington's thinking, vocational progress was more important than political progress. Speaking for black people in his compromise, Washington promised that blacks would remain submissive to whites. He promised to remain loyal to whites. He promised to remain segregated from whites, in all ways that were important to whites. He suggested that black people only wanted the opportunity to demonstrate their usefulness for the economic success of both races and that black people would strive only to gain economic opportunity through industrial training. In return, Washington hoped that whites would make the resources available for black education. The one demand by Washington was for the white power structure to end the racial violence, the lynching of blacks throughout the country. Washington's plea for equity in the Atlanta Compromise speech had little effect on the social structure of American life. As I noted in the introduction, the very next year, 1896, the Supreme Court of the United States handed down a decision upholding the policy of "separate but equal" in the Plessy V. Ferguson landmark case.

---

71 Booker T. Washington, "Up From Slavery," *Commentary* (December 1986), 62-67.

## W.E.B. DUBOIS

DuBois took a very different approach. Not simply concerned with the economic condition of blacks, he sought to bring about a reform in the relationship between blacks and whites. Known primarily as a civil rights activist, he was also a sociologist, historian, and editor. He has been describes as attempting "virtually every possible solution to the problem of twentieth-century racism – scholarship, propaganda, integration, national self-determination, human rights, cultural and economic separatism, politics, international communism, expatriation, third world solidarity."[72] Among his most significant works are The Philadelphia Negro (1899), The Souls of Black Folk (1903), John Brown (1909), Black Reconstruction (1935), and Black Folk, Then and Now (1939). His book The Negro (1915) influenced the work of later Africanist scholars. In his influential work, Black Reconstruction, Du Bois documented how black people were central figures in the American Civil War and Reconstruction.73 He argued that the emancipation of black Americans promoted a radical restructuring of United States society, as well as how and why the country failed to continue support for civil rights for blacks in the aftermath of Reconstruction.

In 1899, W.E.B. DuBois wrote an article entitled "What is the Negro Problem?" in response to the preoccupation with the supposed liabilities of the Negro.[74] In the article, DuBois suggested that the situation for black people in America towards the end of the nineteenth century was not unique. Other nations had conquered their barbarian pasts, making themselves into successful societies, and if other nations did it, America could do the same.

---

72 David Levering Lewis, *W.E.B. Du Bois: The Fight for Equality and the American Century, 1919-1963* (New York: Holt, 2001), 571.

73 For further reading on DuBois, see Elliott M. Rudwick, W.E.B. *Du Bois: Propagandist of the Negro Protest* (New York: Atheneum, 1960) and Robert Gooding-Williams, *In the Shadow of Du Bois: Afro-Modern Political Thought in America* (Cambridge: Harvard University Press, 2009).

74 Eric J. Sundquist, ed., *The Oxford W.E.B. DuBois Reader* (New York: Oxford University Press, 1996), 346.

In response to the commonly held wish among many whites that black would emigrate back to Africa or simply die out because of their genetic inferiority, DuBois held to the notion that black Americans "going away" or "dying out" was not going to happen. So, in order for the nation to be successful, it was going to need to experience a number of reforms. DuBois lays out a number of propositions as axiomatic:

> The Negro is here to stay. It is to the advantage of all, both black and white, that every Negro should make the best of himself. It is the duty of the Negro to raise himself by every effort to the standards of modern civilization and not to lower those standards in any degree. It is the duty of the white people to guard their civilization against debauchment by themselves or others; but in order to do this it is not necessary to hinder and retard the efforts of an earnest people to rise, simply because they lack faith in the ability of that people. With these duties in mind and with a spirit of self-help, mutual aid and co-operation, the two races should strive side by side to realize the ideals of the republic and make this truly a land: of equal opportunity for all men.[75]

DuBois suggested specific contributions needed from both sides of the society, white and black. He laid out, in detail, specific social reforms agendas for each racial group.

### *DuBois' Agenda for Black Americans*

DuBois' believed that the dominant people in the society had a right to demand these reforms from the society's citizens of color. He believed that these demands could be expected even after the dominant group had brutalized its citizens of color. DuBois

75 Ibid., 348-349.

denounced, with no uncertain terms, any doctrine that suggested entitlement other than respect and empowerment:

> That the Negro race has an appalling work of social reform before it need hardly be said. Simply because the ancestors of the present white inhabitants of America went out of their way barbarously to mistreat and enslave the ancestors of the present black inhabitants, gives those blacks no right to ask that the civilization and morality of the land be seriously menaced for their benefit. Men have a right to demand that the members of a civilized community be civilized; that the fabric of human culture, so laboriously woven, be not wantonly or ignorantly destroyed. Consequently a nation may rightly demand, even of a people it has consciously and intentionally wronged, not indeed complete civilization in thirty or one hundred years, but at least every effort and sacrifice possible on their part toward making themselves fit members of the community within a reasonable length of time; that thus they may early become a source of strength and help instead of a national burden.[76]

DuBois came short of the "pull yourselves up by the bootstraps" mentality, but he did hold the Negro responsible for respectful citizenship. "As far as possible and as rapidly as possible the Negro bend his energy to the solving of his own social problems – contributing to his poor, paying his share of the taxes and supporting the schools and public administration."[77] On the other hand, DuBois did not place all of the responsibility on the backs of black people. He managed a balanced approach holding white society responsible for opportunity and empowerment:

> For the accomplishment of this the Negro has a right to demand freedom for self-development, and no more aid from without than is really helpful for furthering that development.

76 Ibid., 349.
77 Ibid., 349.

> Such aid must of necessity be considerable: it must furnish schools and reformatories, and relief and preventive agencies; but the bulk of the work of raising the Negro must be done by the Negro himself, and the greatest help for him will be not to hinder and curtail and discourage his efforts.[78]

Although DuBois does seem to advocate conciliatory behavior, he is not averse to agitation when it is necessary to procure opportunities of advancement: "Against prejudice, injustice and wrong the Negro ought to protest energetically and continuously, but he must never forget that he protests because those things hinder his own efforts, and that those efforts are the key to his future."[79]

After outlining ideas that he calls axiomatic, DuBois goes on in "What is the Negro Problem?" to outline some very specific reforms needed in the black community. These included the following:

> The reduction of crime: In Philadelphia, those efforts should first be directed toward a lessening of Negro crime; no doubt the amount of crime imputed to the race is exaggerated, no doubt features of the Negro's environment over which he has no control, excuse much that is committed; but beyond all this, the amount of crime that can without doubt rightly be laid at the door of the Philadelphia Negro is large and is a menace to a civilized people. Efforts to stop this crime must commence in the Negro homes; they must cease to be, as they often are, breeders of idleness and extravagance and complaint.[80]
>
> Work: Work, continuous and intensive; work, although it be menial and poorly rewarded; work, though done in travail of soul and sweat of brow, must be so impressed upon Negro children as the road to salvation, that a child would feel it a greater disgrace to be idle than to do the humblest

78 Ibid.
79 Ibid.
80 Ibid., 350.

labor...They should be ever encouraged and urged to do so, although they should be taught also that idleness and crime are beneath and not above the lowest work.[81]

Industrial work: It should be the continual object of Negroes to open up better industrial chances for their sons and daughters. Their success here must of course rest largely with the white people, but not entirely. Proper co-operation among forty or fifty thousand colored people ought to open many chances of employment for their sons and daughters in trades, stores and shops, associations and industrial enterprises.[82]

Amusement: Further, some rational means of amusement should be furnished young folks. Prayers meetings and church socials have their place, but they cannot compete in attractiveness with the dance halls and gambling dens of the city. There is a legitimate demand for amusement on the part of the young which may be made a means of education, improvement and recreation. A harmless and beautiful amusement like dancing might with proper effort be rescued from its low and unhealthful associations and made a means of health and recreation. The billiard table is no more wedded to the saloon than to the church if good people did not drive it there. If the Negro homes and churches cannot amuse their young people, and if no other efforts are made to satisfy this want, then we cannot complain if the saloons and clubs and bawdy-houses send these children to crime, disease and death.[83]

Rescue work: There is a vast amount of preventive and rescue work which the Negroes themselves might do: keeping little girls off the street at night, stopping the escorting of unchaperoned young ladies to church and elsewhere, showing the dangers of the lodging system, urging the buying of homes and removal from crowded and tainted neighborhoods, giving lectures and tracts on health and habits, exposing the dangers of gambling and policy-

81 Ibid.
82 Ibid.
83 Ibid., 351.

> playing, and inculcating respect for women. Day-nurseries and sewing-schools, mothers' meetings, the parks and airing places, all these things are little known or appreciated among the masses of Negroes, and their attention should be directed to them.[84]
>
> Better use of money: The spending of money is a matter to which Negroes need to give especial attention. Money is wasted to-day in dress, furniture, elaborate entertainments, costly church edifices, and "insurance" schemes, which ought to go toward buying homes, educating children, giving simple healthful amusement to the young, and accumulating something in the savings bank as against the "insurance" society ought to be started in the Seventh Ward without delay.[85]
>
> Spirit of calm and patience towards fellow citizens: Finally, the Negroes must cultivate a spirit of calm, patient persistence in their attitude toward their fellow citizens rather than of loud and intemperate complaint.[86]

DuBois indicated that one of the most important expectations that he had for black Americans was for the better class of Negros to offer a helping hand to the underclass. In an essay entitled "The Training of Negroes for Social Power" (1903), he developed his understanding of the use of the "Talented Tenth."[87] DuBois said that blacks were responsible for their own social development but they had to have social power available to them to fulfill the task. The responsibility for their own social regeneration ought to be placed largely upon the shoulders of the Negro people. In his view, "such responsibility must carry with it a grant of power; responsibility without power is a mockery and a farce." He contended, "If, therefore, the American people are sincerely anxious that the Negro shall put forth his best efforts to help himself, they must see to it that

84 Ibid., 350.
85 Ibid.
86 Ibid.
87 Ibid., 354ff.

he is not deprived of the freedom and power to strive." He argued further that such "social power" entailed "the growth of initiative among Negroes, the spread of independent thought, the expanding consciousness of manhood."[88]

DuBois understood that education was an important key if the Negro was going to move along the path of self-development. However, for DuBois, education was more important than simply becoming literate. Education meant that black people would be trained in the classics of the world in order to understand the ways of the world. DuBois was not satisfied with industrial education. He believed that blacks should be allowed to develop well-trained minds with intellectual power and leadership. The Negro problem, it has often been said, is largely a problem of ignorance – not simply of illiteracy, but a deeper ignorance of the world and its ways, of the thought and experience of men – an ignorance of self and possibilities of human souls. This can be overcome only by training. This training must take the form of social leadership that he considered a primary part of the education process. DuBois observed that the history of advanced civilizations proved that it was necessary to have "well-trained minds...and this power of intellectual leadership." This, to DuBois' understanding, would be the task of the talented tenth among American Negroes. This step would be necessary before the black race could be expected "to assume the responsibility of dispelling its own ignorance."[89]

DuBois believed that better developed public school systems would be necessary for the task of educating the Negro masses.

> The very first step toward the settlement of the Negro problem is the spread of intelligence. The first step toward wider intelligence is a free public-school system; and the

88 Ibid., 355.
89 Ibid., 356.

> first and most important step toward a public-school system is the equipment and adequate support of a sufficient number of Negro colleges. . . . Below the colleges and connected with them must come the normal and high schools, judiciously distributed and carefully manned.[90]

His outline suggested that this system needed to support a sufficient number of Negro colleges as well as a systemic attempt to organize secondary education.

### *DuBois' Agenda for White Americans*

DuBois understood the condition of the masses of black people in America as a condition that he characterized as poor, ignorant, and inefficient. DuBois began his list of expectations from the white community by urging them to face that reality and shoulder the responsibility:

> Today, however, we must face the fact that a natural repugnance to close intermingling with unfortunate ex-slaves has descended to a discrimination that very seriously hinders them from being anything better. It is right and proper to object to ignorance and consequently to ignorant men; but if by our actions we have been responsible for their ignorance and are still actively engaged in keeping them ignorant, the argument loses its moral force. So with the Negroes: men have a right to object to a race so poor and ignorant and inefficient as the mass of the Negroes; but if their policy in the past is parent of much of this condition, and if to-day by shutting black boys and girls out of most avenues of decent employment they are increasing pauperism and vice, then they must hold themselves largely responsible for the deplorable results.[91]

90 Ibid., 356-357.
91 Ibid., 352.

DuBois undoubtedly had the failed Freedman's Bureau in mind when he suggested the involvement of the United States government in the development of the education system. He suggested, without apology, that money needed for these objectives could and should come from the government as well as private philanthropy:

> Whence, now, is the money coming for this educational system? For the common schools the support should come from local communities, the State governments, and the United States Government; for secondary education, support should come from local and State governments and private philanthropy; for the colleges, from private philanthropy and the United States Government. I make no apology for bringing the United States Government in thus conspicuously. The General Government must give aid to Southern education if illiteracy and ignorance are to cease threatening the very foundations of civilization within any reasonable time.[92]

In addition to the need to provide educational opportunities, DuBois insisted that white people stop the discriminating policies that barred Negroes from earning a decent living. Further, the white community needed to expand the opportunities for work. DuBois believed the policies of his time to be morally wrong. He presented the argument that holding blacks back from jobs and opportunities for education was not only hurting the black community but it was to the advantage of the white community to empower blacks for self-development:

> There is no doubt that in Philadelphia the centre and kernel of the Negro problem as-far-as the white people are concerned is the narrow opportunities afforded Negroes for earning a decent living. Such discrimination is morally wrong, politically dangerous, industrially wasteful, and socially silly. It is the duty of the whites to stop it, and to do so primarily

92 Ibid., 357.

> for their own sake. Industrial freedom of opportunity has by long experience been proven to be generally best for all. Moreover the cost of crime and pauperism, the growth of slums, and the pernicious influences of idleness and lewdness, cost the public far more than would the hurt to the feelings of a carpenter to work beside a black man, or a shop-girl to stand beside a darker mate.[93]

Even as DuBois urged whites to open up job opportunities for blacks, he tried to address the fears of many whites by suggesting that this would not mean taking jobs and food out of the mouths of white people.

Even more importantly, DuBois is not advocating an affirmative action program that amounted to quotas. He wanted black people to be hired based on their merit, talented and abilities to do the work for which they were qualified. He did not call for the "wholesale replacing of white workmen for Negroes out of sympathy or philanthropy." He did argue, however, "talent should be rewarded, and aptness used in commerce and industry whether its owner be black or white." He contended that "the same incentive to good, honest, effective work be placed before a black office boy as before a white one – before a black porter as before a white one; and that unless this is done the city has no right to complain that black boys lose interest in work and drift into idleness and crime." For this reason, he urged that "leaders of industry and opinion" try their best "to open up new opportunities and give new chances to bright colored boys."[94]

In sum, DuBois urged the white community not to draw their conclusions about the nature of the black community from their observations of the underclass of the black community but to recognize and to develop a cooperative relationship with member of

---

93 Ibid., 352.
94 Ibid., 352.

the better class of Negroes. In their efforts to uplift "the Negro," the people of Philadelphia "must recognize the existence of the better class of Negroes and must gain their active aid and co-operation by generous and polite conduct." This "better class of Negroes," he argued, did not want "help or pity." What they wanted was "a generous recognition of their difficulties, and a broad sympathy with the problem of life as it presents itself to them."[95]

### *Agitation versus Conciliation*

A close look at the efforts of DuBois has him, at times, looking somewhat conciliatory. He often came to the table with requests and suggestions rather than demands for the white community designed to affect social justice. However, in his address to the Niagara Movement in 1905 and his letters to President Harding in 1921, his conciliatory tone had clearly changed to what would characterize agitation. The Niagara Movement was the original name for what latter become known as The National Association for the Advancement of Colored People (NAACP). I quote below the main concerns found in this declaration under the various principles each statement seeks to uphold:

> Progress: The members of the conference, known as the Niagara Movement, assembled in annual meeting at Buffalo, July 11th, 1905, congratulate the Negro-Americans on certain undoubted evidences of progress in the last decade, particularly the increase of intelligence, the buying of property, the checking of crime, the uplift in home life, the advance in literature and art, and the demonstration of constructive and executive ability in the conduct of great religious, economic, and educational institutions.

95 Ibid., 353-354.

Suffrage: At the same time, we believe that this class of American citizens should protest emphatically and continually against the curtailment of their political rights. We believe in manhood suffrage; we believe that no man is so good, intelligent or wealthy as to be entrusted wholly with the welfare of his neighbor.

Civil Liberty: We believe also in protest against the curtailment of our civil rights. All American citizens have the right to equal treatment in places of public entertainment according to their behavior and deserts.

Economic Opportunity: We especially complain against the denial of equal opportunities to us in economic life; in the rural districts of the South this amounts to peonage and virtual slavery; all over the South it tends to crush labor and small business enterprises; and everywhere American prejudice, helped often by iniquitous laws, is making it more difficult for Negro-Americans to earn a decent living.

Education: Common school education should be free to all American children and compulsory. High school training should be adequately provided for all, and college training should be the monopoly of no class or race in any section of our common country. We believe that, in defense of our own institutions, the United States should aid common school education, particularly in the South, and we especially recommend concerted agitation to this end. We urge an increase in public high school facilities in the South, where the Negro-Americans are almost wholly without such provisions. We favor well-equipped trade and technical schools for the training of artisans, and the need of adequate and liberal endowment for a few institutions of higher education must be patent to sincere well-wishers of the race.

Courts: We demand upright judges in courts, juries selected without discrimination on account of color and the same measure of punishment and the same efforts at reformation for black as for white offenders. We need orphanages and farm schools for dependent children, juvenile reformatories for delinquents, and the abolition of the dehumanizing convict-lease system.

Public Opinion: We note with alarm the evident retrogression in this of land of sound public opinion on the subject of manhood rights, republican government and human brotherhood, and we pray God that this nation will not degenerate into a mob of boasters and oppressors, but rather will return to the faith of the fathers, that all men were created free and equal, with certain unalienable rights.

Health: We plead for health – for an opportunity to live in decent houses and localities, for a chance to rear our children in physical and moral cleanliness.

Employers and Labor Unions: We hold up for public execration the conduct of two opposite classes of men: The practice among employers of importing ignorant Negro-Americans laborers in emergencies, and then affording them neither protection nor permanent employment, and the practice of labor unions in proscribing and boycotting and oppressing thousands of their fellow-toilers, simply because they are black. These methods have accentuated and will accentuate the war of labor and capital, and they are disgraceful to both sides.

Protest: We refuse to allow the impression to remain that the Negro-American assents to inferiority, is submissive under oppression and apologetic before insults. Through helplessness we may submit, but the voice of protest of ten million Americans must never cease to assail the ears of their fellows, so long as America is unjust.

Color-Line: Any discrimination based simply on race or color is barbarous, we care not how hallowed it be by custom expediency or prejudice. Differences made on account of ignorance, immorality, or disease are legitimate methods of fighting evil, and against them we have no word of protest, but discriminations based simply and solely on physical peculiarities, place of birth, color of skin, are relics of that unreasoning human savagery of which the world is and ought to be thoroughly ashamed.

"Jim Crow" Cars: We protest against the "Jim Crow" car, since its effect is and must be to make us pay first-class fare for third-class accommodations, render us open to insults and discomfort and to crucify wantonly our womanhood and self-respect.

Soldiers: We regret that his nation has never seen fit adequately to reward the black soldiers who, in its five wars, have defended their county with their blood, and yet have been systematically denied the promotions which their abilities deserve. And we regard as unjust, the exclusion of black boys from the military and naval training schools.

War Amendments: We urge upon Congress the enactment of appropriate legislation for securing the proper enforcement of those articles of freedom, the thirteenth, fourteenth and fifteenth amendments of the Constitution of the United States.

Oppression: We repudiate the monstrous doctrine that the oppressor should be the sole authority as to the rights of the oppressed. The Negro race in America stolen, ravished and degraded, struggling up through difficulties and oppression, needs sympathy and receives criticism: needs help and is given hindrance, needs protection and is given mob-violence, needs justice and is given charity, needs leadership and is given cowardice and apology, needs bread and is given a stone. This nation will never stand justified before God until these things are changed.

The Church: Especially are we surprised and astonished at the recent attitude of the church of Christ-- of an increase of a desire to bow to racial prejudice, to narrow the bounds of human brotherhood, and to segregate black men to some outer sanctuary. This is wrong, unchristian and disgraceful to the twentieth century civilization.

Agitation: Of the above grievance we do not hesitate to

complain, and to complain loudly and insistently. To ignore, overlook, or apologize for these wrongs is to prove ourselves unworthy of freedom. Persistent manly agitation is the way to liberty, and toward this goal the Niagara Movement has started and asks the cooperation of all men of all races.

Help: At the same time we want to acknowledge with deep thankfulness the help of our fellowmen from the Abolitionists down to those who today still stand for equal opportunity and who have given and still give of their wealth and of their poverty for our advancement.

Duties: And while we are demanding and ought to demand, and will continue to demand the rights enumerated above, God forbid that we should ever forget to urge corresponding duties upon our people:

The duty to vote.

The duty to respect the rights of others.

The duty to work.

The duty to obey the laws.

The duty to be clean and orderly.

The duty to send our children to school.

The duty to respect ourselves, even as we respect others.

This statement, complaint and prayer we submit to the American people, and Almighty God.[96]

The language in this document communicates the clear intention of the organization to press the issues. DuBois made his case for the principles that would undergird the NAACP with strong words: "American citizens should protest emphatically and continually" (the "Suffrage" principle); "We believe also in protest against the curtailment of our civil rights" (the "Civil Liberty" principle); "We especially complain against the denial of economic opportunity" (the

96 "The Niagara Movement Declaration of Principles," in Quintard Taylor, ed., *African American History of Western New York,* http://www.math.buffalo.edu/~sww/0history/hwny-niagara-movement.html (accessed June 28, 2008).

"Economic Opportunity" principle). These are strong words, indeed. His intention to forgo conciliation is most clear in what he called the "Courts" principle: "We demand upright judges in courts, juries selected without discrimination."[97]

Later, in his *Address to the Country* (1906), issued at the second conference, Harper's Ferry, West Virginia, he outlined five objectives for black Americans:

> First, we would vote; with the right to vote goes everything: Freedom, manhood, the honor of your wives, the chastity of your daughters, the right to work, and the chance to rise, and let no man listen to those who deny this.
>
> Second, we want discrimination in public accommodation to cease. Separation in railway and street cars, based simply on race and color, is un-American, un-democratic, and silly. We protest against all such discrimination.
>
> Third, we claim the right of freemen to walk, talk, and be with them that wish to be with us. No man has a right to choose another man's friends, and to attempt to do so is an impudent interference with the most fundamental human privilege.
>
> Fourth, we want the laws enforced against rich as well as poor; against Capitalist as well as Laborer; against white as well as black. We are not more lawless than the white race, we are more often arrested, convicted, and mobbed. We want justice even for criminals and outlaws. We want the Constitution of the country enforced. We want Congress to take charge of Congressional elections. We want the Fourteenth amendment carried out to the letter and every State disfranchised in Congress which attempts to disfranchise its rightful voters. We want the Fifteenth amendment enforced and No State allowed to base its franchise simply on color.

97 Ibid.

> Fifth, we want our children educated. The school system in the country districts of the South is a disgrace and in few towns and cities are Negro schools what they ought to be. We want the national government to step in and wipe out illiteracy in the South. Either the United States will destroy ignorance or ignorance will destroy the United States.[98]

Moreover, in an open letter to President Warren Harding, written in March of 1921, DuBois outlined his expectations for white society in general and the president specifically. I quote the body of the letter:

> By an unprecedented vote you have been called to the most powerful position in thc gift of mankind. Of the more than hundred million human beings whose destiny rests so largely with you in the next four years, one in every ten is of Negro descent.
>
> Your enemies in the campaign sought to count you among this number and if it were true it would give us deep satisfaction to welcome you to the old and mystic chrism of Negroland, whence many mighty souls have stepped since time began.
>
> But blood and physical descent are little and idle things as compared with spiritual heritage. And here we would see you son of the highest: a child of Abraham Lincoln and Lloyd Garrison and Frederick Douglass; a grandson of Thomas Jefferson and John Quincy Adams; and a lineal descendant of the martyred Fathers of the Free of all times and lands.
>
> We appeal to you: we the outcast and lynched, the mobbed and murdered, the despoilcd and insulted; and yet withal, the indomitable, unconquered, unbending and unafraid black children of kings and slaves and of the best blood of the workers of the earth –
>
> WE WANT THE RIGHT TO VOTE. WE WANT TO TRAVEL WITHOUT INSULT. WE WANT LYNCHING

98 Ibid.

AND MOB-LAW QUELLED FOREVER. WE WANT FREEDOM FOR OUR BROTHERS IN HAITI.

We know that the power to do these things is not entirely in your hands, but its beginnings lie there. After the fourth of March, on you more than on any other human being rests the redemption of the blood of Africa and through it the peace of the world. All the cruelty, rape and atrocities of slavery; all the groans and humiliations of half-freedom; all the theft and degradation of that spirit of the Klu Klux mob that seeks to build a free America on racial, religious and class hatred – the weight of all this woe is yours.

You, Sir, whether you will or no, stand responsible. You are responsible for the truth back of the pictures of the burning of Americans circulated in European drawing-rooms; for the spectacle of 82% of the voters of the South disfranchised under a government called a democracy; for the hypocrisy of a nation seeking to lend idealism to the world for peace when within its own borders thee is more murder, theft, riot and crucifixion than was ever even charged against Bolshevik Russia.

In the name of our fathers, President Harding, our fathers black and white who toiled and bled and died to make this a free and decent nation, will you not tear aside the cobwebs of politics, and lies of society, and the grip of industrial thieves, and give us an administration which will say and mean: *the first and fundamental and inescapable problem of American democracy is Justice to the American Negro.* If races cannot live together in peace and happiness in America, they cannot live together in the world. Race isolation died a century ago. Human unity within and without Nations, must and will succeed—and you, Sir, must start bringing this to pass.[99]

The language in this letter is clearly language of demand and

99 W.E.B. DuBois, "An Open Letter to Warren Gamaliel Harding," TeachingAmerican History .org (1921; Ashbrook Center for Public Affairs at Ashland University, 2006), http://www.teachingamericanhistory.org/library/index.as;?documentprint=1118 (accessed June 28, 2008).

desperation. It is a desperation also felt and voiced by Washington but more strongly addressed by DuBois. It is a desperation that is finally played out during the rest of the twentieth century through the race riots after WWI to the civil rights movement of the fifties and sixties to the race riots in 1968 and 1992.

Later, DuBois outlined the idea that blacks wanted social equality in an article entitled "President Harding and Social Equality."[100] He wrote the article in response to a speech given by Harding where the president argued in support of social equality between blacks and whites. DuBois found it necessary to clarify and qualify Harding's speech. He did so by defining social equality in two ways. The obvious and clear meaning is the right of a human being to accept companionship with his fellow on terms of equal and reciprocal courtesy.[101] The second meaning that DuBois wanted people to understand when he spoke of social equality had to do with a distinction between (1) "the eligibility to association with men" and (2) "the forced and illogical meaning" having to with "the right to demand private association with any particular person." The demand, he argued, was "idiotic" and "was never made by an sane person." On the contrary, he contended, "for any person to admit that his character is such that he is physically and morally unfit to talk or travel or eat with his fellow men, or that he has no desire to associate with decent people, would be an admission which none but a leper, a criminal or a liar could possibly make." It is the "very essence of self respect and human equality and it carries with it no jot of arrogance or assumption – it is simply Homo Sum."[102] In making this distinction, DuBois wanted to distinguish between the "eligibility to associate" and the "right to demand the association." He is saying that the association should be something that comes

100 W.E.B. DuBois, "President Harding and Social Equality," *TeachingAmericanHistory.org*, (accessed September 9, 2008).

101 Ibid.

102 Ibid.

naturally. Nobody wants to associate with people who are flawed in character but blacks of good moral character should not have to accept a white person's imposition of undesirability as if the person were a leper, a criminal, or a liar when that determination is made solely on the color of one's skin.

## WASHINGTON AND DUBOIS AND THE PROBLEMS OF RACISM AND RACIALIZATION

How are we to evaluate the contributions to Washington and DuBois to the critique of racism and racialization in American society? In the last section of this chapter, I seek to discuss their influence on our understanding of the problem of racism, on the one hand, and the problem of racialization, on the other.

### *A Brief Historical Sketch of Washington's and DuBois' Influence on the Problem of Racism*

We begin by discussing how they influenced black Americans in their struggle against racism in American society. To guide us in this assessment, I quote Glenn Loury, who summarizes what he considers the two major strategies employed by black people in their fight for social justice since the *reconstruction project* of the middle to the late nineteenth century. The context for his summary is a comparison between the perspectives of supreme justices, Clarence Thomas and Thurgood Marshall. Reflecting on the "conflict between Thomas's black supporters and his black critics," he states that this conflict "recalls to mind the epochal struggle over public ideas among blacks that raged at the turn of the century between the followers, respectively, of Booker T. Washington and of

W.E.B. Du Bois."[103] In his description of this "epochal struggle," Loury suggests that although Washington's more conciliatory view of black and white relationships would be "orthodoxy" for black Americans until his death in 1915, it was finally DuBois' more reformist stance that won the day for the twentieth century with the formation of the NAACP in 1909. On the one hand, Loury notes, Washington's view was "the orthodoxy" for black Americans while he lived. "He expended considerable energies to ensure that this was so, using his far-reaching influence among whites to cut off his critics from sources of financial support." On the hand, Loury goes on, "in the end the ideas of the Du Bois camp prevailed, leading to the founding of the National Association for the Advancement of Colored People and providing the impetus for the decades-long legal struggle that culminated in the Brown decision, which was successfully argued before the Supreme Court by Thurgood Marshall."[104] Writing in 1995, Loury suggested that the "DuBois/Marshall" position had taken over as the orthodox position.

As Loury also points out, there were, of course, other points of view, during the same time, besides the ones held by Washington and DuBois. It is hard to draw a clear line among the various movements determining where agitation ends and accommodation begins. There seems to have been more of a continuum between these positions. Early on, the NAACP was considered the agitator; later on in the dialogue, the NAACP members were considered part of the accommodating group. During this period, for example, there were a number of leaders who supported a Black Nationalist position. This position was principally the movement for the emigration of black people to establish a colony in Liberia. There was some overlap of ideas but the influence of Washington or DuBois was small. The

103 Glenn C. Loury, ed., *One by One from the Inside Out: Essays and Reviews on Race and Responsibility in America* (New York: The Free Press, 1995), 65.
104 Ibid., 65.

most well known among these leaders are Bishop Henry M. Turner, Monroe Trotter, and Marcus Mosiah Garvey.

Turner in some ways would be considered a Washingtonite. He agreed with Washington on a number of important points. Yet, when all was said and done, he was one of the most aggressive of the agitators. In 1895, Turner could have challenged Washington for the mantel of black leadership. However, he was more interested in getting out of the country than establishing himself as the leader of social reform. Yet, even in this, Loury points out, Turner was "not a stranger to certain key aspects of Washington's thought." He also emphasized "people raising themselves up by their own bootstraps" and he concentrated on "agricultural and mechanical arts as the prerequisite to economic independence". In these respects, Turner and Washington understood one another well.[105] Yet, later on in his career, Turner would have to be considered an agitator. At the end of the century, "when white hostility was greater than at any other period in American history, Turner's tower of strength was his willingness to take a public offensive." Loury points out that Turner refused to "bow before the canons of respectability at a time when whites were all too willing to require blacks to grin and bear it while they turned the screws of oppression with the greatest dignity and pious pretense." Not only did he refuse "to play that game and struck out mercilessly against hypocrisy and deception," but he was also, "as a matter of fact, not beyond violence" and in a Voice of Missions editorial urged that "Negroes Get Guns" to defend themselves against the lynch mobs.[106] To what degree Turner was influenced by Washington and DuBois may be unclear. It is clear however, that at different points in Turner's life he took on each of the positions of his predecessors with both concession and agitation as they seemed appropriate for the circumstances.

105 Ibid., 165.
106 Ibid.

In turn, Garvey is considered the last of the great emigrationist leaders. He was invited to lecture in the United State by invitation of Booker T. Washington. But by the time Garvey actually started his lecturing career in 1916 Washington had already died. By 1920, during Garvey's prominence, he sounded more like DuBois than he did like Washington. Although Garvey was critical of preachers as "so-called leaders of the race" who persuaded their people to postpone the blessings of this life for a future paradise, he did not mount a direct assault upon religion, or upon the black religious establishment.[107] Although there were other black leaders and although the lines are not clear in terms of the influence of Washington or DuBois, by far the most influential positions of those days were led by Booker T. Washington and W.E.B. DuBois. The influence on Garvey is no exception.

During the first two decades of the twentieth century, Washington's doctrine of gradualism, accommodation, and segregation was championed by both blacks and whites. It can probably be said that most people supported his position. Washington's position was even quoted by President Warren Harding, who used him as support for the argument for segregation between whites and blacks. A number of books were being written during this time period providing literary and intellectual support for segregation: Charles Carroll's *The Negro a Beast* (1900); William P. Calhoun's *The Caucasian and the Negro* (1902); William B. Smith's *The Color Line* (1905); Robert Shufeldt's *The Negro: A Menace to American Civilization* (1907); and Madison Grant's *The Passing of the Great Race* (1916). White racists used these works and others to arouse public support for stemming the tide of immigration with the Quota Act of 1921 and for keeping blacks in their places. The enormous popularity of this literature even reached the White House, where Warren G. Harding quoted Lothrop Stoddard's *The Rising Tide of Color Against White*

---

107 Ibid., 178.

*World Supremacy* in support of Booker T. Washington's doctrine of social separation.[108]

How was Washington's position viewed among blacks during this period? If whites like Harding found Washington's doctrine of social separation amenable to them, then at about the time of race riots of 1917 and 1919, some blacks found it necessary to abandon "the pacifism and gradualism" their preachers espoused and become more "aggressive." The reason for this was that most church members drew back from the hard line of Bishop Turner and others like him and instead "enlisted in church programs for community betterment, cultural enrichment, and only mild opposition to the most destructive aspects of white racism."[109]

Thus, although opposed by those who were not moved by his call for personal advancement, Washington's gradualism was adopted by most black preachers. These preachers were attracted to his position not only because "they lacked the courage to fight back," but also because they found it "consonant with the ethics of the white Christianity" that was having an influence on them. The picture of "the nonviolent, self-effacing, patiently-suffering white Jesus" held up by the conservative evangelicals and revivalists at the turn of the century became for many black preachers the authoritative image of what it is like to be a Christian. Ostensibly supported by Scripture, that image provided many black church leaders with irrefutable confirmation of the "wisdom and expediency of Washington's position."[110] In effect, the Washington doctrine assimilated by white Christianity had been processed in such a way as to pacify the black church.

The development of the NAACP cannot be divorced from the influence of the black church. As I have discussed, under the influence

108 Ibid., 168.
109 Ibid., 169.
110 Ibid., 168.

of DuBois, the NAACP had started as an organization with a vision to aggressively confront the racism and other injustices of the day. Over time, however, it became more complacent to the conditions in the black communities. A number of reasons contributed to this shift in the organization. First, from its inception there was a heavy influence from the white community. Secondly, the black church and clergy made up the backbone of the organization. It has been said that *the black church is the NAACP on its knees.* DuBois regarded the Council of Bishops of the AME Church as the most powerful and prestigious group of men in black America. Third, the more affluent black churches began to acquiesce to the white version of Christianity.

In addition, the middle class Black Bourgeoisie was not willing to embrace the radicalism of the NAACP's past. As Gayraud Wilmore has pointed out, the blame for this turn away from a more assertive confrontation with racism cannot be placed entirely upon the clergy. In his words, "The push and pull of secularized white urban society permeated the ghetto and drew the best prepared and most enterprising of the migrants irresistibly toward the norms and lifestyles that Frazier described in Black Bourgeoisie." Black ministers may have been deeply troubled about the direction of "Bookerism," especially as they "faced with the necessity of orienting their congregations to the requirements of city life." Nonetheless, they could not successfully hold back "a deradicalization process without breaking with orthodox Christianity, as they understood and believed it." Moreover, Loury goes on, "the powerful white influence within the early NAACP and other groups with which the churches were allied also drew the community into a comfortable accommodation with the white middle class and mainline Protestantism." These ministers had little choice but "to go along with their people if they were to remain within the orbit of acceptable social policy and political behavior." No longer a "primarily lower-class institution arbitrating the terms of black existence," the church "was becoming thoroughly middle-class."[111]

By the mid-fifties, the black church, by many accounts, had become almost irrelevant in terms of its willingness and ability to fight for social justice, and the NAACP was being considered by many to be an organization of Uncle Toms. After graduating from Boston University with a Doctor of Philosophy, Martin Luther King came on the scene with the ability, as Wilmore says, quoting Lerone Bennett, to "translate religious fervor into social action, thereby creating political leadership under the rubric of his religious ministry under conditions of extreme danger and liability."[112] On a national level, he was able to change the image of the black church. On an institutional level, he was able to create new legitimacy for the NAACP. King managed to make progress for black people in the area of social justice by blending DuBois' agitation with a Hegelian philosophy of dialectical process and Gandhi's nonviolence.

However, despite victories in several Southern cities, the development of a number of effective spin-off student movements, and the creation of pressure put on the congress and president of the United States to pass a half dozen civil rights laws (including the landmark Brown case), Adam Clayton Powell, Jr. and other black leaders took critical positions against the NAACP and King. As early as 1963, Powell, a New York congressman and Harlem pastor, began to attack the NAACP and, somewhat less vociferously, King himself, for what Powell considered acquiescence to the white liberal establishment. In May 1965 at a Chicago rally Powell spoke of "black power" as indispensable for the black community. On May 29, 1966, he declared in a baccalaureate address at Howard University that "Human rights are God-given. Civil rights are man-

111 Gayraud S. Wilmore, *Black Religion and Black Radicalism: An Interpretation of the Religious History of African Americans*, 3rd ed. (New York: Orbis, 2003), 173-174.
112 Ibid., 204.

made." We must commit our lives, he argued, "to implement human rights." For us "to demand these God-given rights," he maintained, "is to seek black power—the power to build black institutions of splendid achievement."[113]

Powell's address at Howard was heard by Stokely Carmichael, then a leader in the Student Non-Violent Coordination Committee (SNCC), the right arm organization for the Southern Christian Leadership Conference led by Martin Luther King. Shortly after Powell's address at Howard, Carmichael, already having grown disillusioned with the non-violent strategies employed by King, made his break from King. By 1967, it was becoming increasingly clear that the nonviolence-espousing hegemony of the NAACP and religious groups over the black revolution had fallen out of phase with a new development that was primarily northern-based, cultural as well as political, self-righteously secular, and alienated from traditional American values and the quest for black civil rights. By late 1967, the SNCC had completed an alliance with revolutionary movements outside the United States and was deep into a relationship with the independence movement in Puerto Rico and with Fidel Castro in Cuba. Carmichael was the new prophet of a resurgent radicalism, although he was soon upstaged by his SNCC associate H. Rap Brown, who was even more committed to breaking out of the moralistic restraints of the civil rights organizations and the churches. By the time of King's death, in 1968, Carmichael had aligned himself with H. Rap Brown, Huey P. Newton, Bobby Seale, and with the most aggressive form of social agitation in the *Black Panther Party for Self-Defense*. From the late 1960s on, the generally accepted doctrine for racial progress had moved from a Washingtonian model to following the DuBois model of agitation.

113 Ibid., 210.

However, by the 1980s this doctrine as the unquestioned position by black leadership had begun to change. Glenn Loury represents the new black intellectual who has moved away from the DuBois doctrine and is re-embracing the Washington position. Loury observes: "Of course, the Du Bois–Marshall view is today's orthodoxy, an orthodoxy defended fiercely by the civil rights establishment from the criticism of radical dissidents (like Thomas) just as Washington defended his, and with similar methods." Nonetheless, he goes on to observe that "there are signs that a new era is dawning, and that in the contemporary struggle over which ideas will inform efforts to improve the black condition into the twenty-first century, the principles laid down by Booker T. Washington will be rediscovered and play an important role." Indeed, this is what he argues for himself. [114] He urges that the time for agitation has passed. He insists that the conditions for equality of citizenship have come. The remaining issues lie within the communities of color as pathological problems with people of color holding the keys to their solution. On the one hand, he notes that "it cannot be said that history has proven Washington right and Du Bois wrong in their debate about what blacks should have done nearly a century ago." Nonetheless, given the way the history of black Americans has evolved, it appears that "the animating spirit of Booker T. Washington's philosophy offers a sounder guide to the future for blacks than that reflected in the worldview of his critics." The "problem of second-class political status for blacks," which Du Bois devoted much of his life to fighting against, "has been resolved." But "the problem of underdevelopment – the "brains, property, and character" problem that Washington spent a lifetime trying to address – remains very much with us." Loury goes on, "Full equality of social standing in American society, the goal that blacks now seek, can never be attained until the fact of black underdevelopment is squarely faced and reversed.

114 Loury, *One by One from the Inside*, 66.

As Washington grasped intuitively, equality of this sort rests more on the performance of blacks in the economic and social sphere than it does on the continued expansion of legal rights."[115] Loury is not alone in his opinion. Among those who would generally agree with him are Clarence Thomas, Thomas Sowell, Shellby Steele, Ward Connerly and Bill Cosby.

## DUBOIS AND THE QUESTION OF RACIALIZATION

So far in this chapter, I have discussed how Washington's calls for economic reforms and DuBois' calls for a more profound legal equality between the races provided a powerful critique of racism in American society, albeit in different ways. In this final section, I deal with the problem of racialization (as defined in my introduction to this book). I will focus my discussion on DuBois' response to this problem because, of these two leaders, he dealt most extensively with the question of Negro racial identity. His complex treatment of the question of racialization gives us insight into the deep interconnection and yet difference between the critique of racism, on the one hand, and the question of racial identity, on the other.

Thomas Gossett tells us that by the 1920s there was plenty of evidence concluding that racial categories were social constructs and that theories of the superiority of one race over another were neither valid nor scientifically reliable. Yet, many continued to classify and to describe human beings according to so-called "races." As Gossett has observed, even though many scientists of the early twentieth century did not accept a biological typology for categorizing the races, they were still caught up emotionally in the dialogue about race. We now generally accept the premise that attempts to construct any theory of history or civilization upon "racial theory" – that

115 Ibid., 68-69.

is, "attempts to describe accurately the differences of character, temperament, and intelligence among the races" – have been "failures." We acknowledge that "race theory" has frequently lent itself to "the crudest kind of manipulation by the people who wished to justify a scheme of exploitation or discrimination." Nonetheless, it was not until the 1920s that racists first met a serious check from the sciences and the academic disciplines. We can hardly help but wonder – now that the claims of the racists are widely recognized as having little or no scientific backing – why the opposition to racism was so long in developing. As Gossett asks, "Were not the effusions of the nineteenth-century racists, for example, extreme enough to call for a more sober scrutiny among serious thinkers?"[116] One reason, he suggests, is that the scientists themselves frequently spoke of race in "personal and emotional tones rather than in terms of fact." There are few subjects that involve more "prejudice," he suggests, than that of race. Unlike religious, political, or social ideas, those "differences" we have chosen to call "racial differences" are what we have been born with; they cannot change. Gossett notes, "We all belong to one race or another or to a combination of races, and thus all of us are involved to some extent in an emotional attachment to the idea that our own race is at least potentially equal to others." Our debates over the "merits and defects of races" take place in "a peevish and ill-tempered atmosphere," one in which the opponents frequently "get personal" and "tell members of other races home truths about themselves." Indeed, he observes, "the usual response to the racist attack has been for the victim to reply in kind against the race of his opponent – not to question the dogma of racism."[117]

Gossett suggests that even DuBois fell into the trap of defining people according to racial lines: "The Negro leader, W.E.B. DuBois,

116 Thomas F. Gossett, *Race: The History of an Idea in America (*New York: Oxford Press, 1997), 409.

117 Ibid., 409-410.

in bitterness and frustration over prejudice against members of his race, responded at one point by appealing to the counter-racism based upon the supposed superiority of Negroes to whites."[118] In a similar vein, Eric Sundquist's editorial comments to the first chapter of his *Oxford Reader* suggest that DuBois recognized early on that "the ambiguities and complexities of race as a category were responsible for the misuse of race in scientific and political theory." He suggests that, having inherited the prevailing nineteenth century belief in "racialism"—the view that people belong to broad, often national groups defined by shared physical, emotional, and intellectual traits – DuBois never quite discarded his own initial view that race had some "biological" basis. Instead, he "constantly refined his own definitions over time, arguing more clearly that race must be understood principally as cultural and political concept."[119]

In his article entitled "The Conservation of Races," it is clear that DuBois had reviewed the scientific literature on race theory. He mentioned many of the theories in his article and named several of the leading race scientists including Thomas Henry Huxley, Friedrich Ratzel as well as Johann-Friedrich Blumenbach and Charles Darwin. On the one hand, he concludes that "race science" comes short of giving definitive answers to the common questions being asked. "All these physical characteristics are patent enough," he observes, "and if they agreed with each other it would be very easy to classify mankind. Unfortunately for scientists, however, these criteria of race are most exasperatingly intermingled. Color does not agree with texture of hair, for many of the dark races have straight hair; nor does color agree with the breadth of the head, for the yellow Tartar has a broader head than the German; nor, again, has the science of language as yet succeeded in clearing up the relative

118 Ibid., 410.
119 Sundquist, ed., *The Oxford W.E.B. DuBois Reader*, 37.

authority of these various and contradictory criteria."[120] On the other hand, although DuBois concludes that racial typology cannot be substantiated by science, in the end, he still assumes some of the prevailing ideas around race theory to have validity: "The final word of science, so far, is that we have at least two, perhaps three, great families of human beings—the whites and Negroes, possibly the yellow race. That other races have arisen from the intermingling of the blood of these two."[121]

DuBois draws his conclusions from two observations. First, people look different from one another. The difference in appearance can be collected into groups. He observes: "Although the wonderful developments of human history teach that the grosser physical differences of color, hair and bone go but a short way toward explaining the different roles which groups of men have played in human progress, yet there are differences—subtle, delicate and elusive, though they may be—which have silently but definitely separated men into groups." And these differences are clearly defined: "While these subtle forces have generally followed the natural cleavage of common blood, descent and physical peculiarities, they have at other times swept across and ignored these. At all times, however, they have divided human beings into races, which, while they perhaps transcend scientific definition, nevertheless, are clearly defined to the eye of the historian and sociologist."[122]

Second, in addition to the way people look, race or racial groups have historically played a role in terms of the contributions different groups of people make to the greater society. These observations, in DuBois' view, cannot be ignored: "If this be true, then the history of the world is the history, not of individuals, but of groups, not of nations, but of races, and he who ignores or seeks

120 Ibid., 39.
121 Ibid.
122 Ibid., 40.

to override the race idea in human history ignores and overrides the central thought of all history." But if race cannot be ignored, then, "What, then, is a race?" In his view it is "a vast family of human beings, generally of common blood and language, always of common history, traditions and impulses, who are both voluntarily and involuntarily striving together for the accomplishment of certain more or less vividly conceived ideals of life." When we look at history, he observes, "there can be no doubt, first, as to the widespread, nay, universal, prevalence of the race idea, the race spirit, the race ideal, and as to its efficiency as the vastest and most ingenious invention for human progress."[123]

DuBois goes further than merely accepting the idea that we can type people according to race. He also accepted the idea, as reality, that personal and corporate character was implicitly embedded in racial groups. Not only were groups and nations differentiated by "blood, color and cranial measurements," but also deeper distinctions – also physically based – could be found in spiritual and psychic differences among the nations. These personal and corporate or national traits produced what he calls a "message." This "message" is the contribution that each of these groups manages to make to the greater civilization. But while race differences have followed mainly physical race lines, yet no mere physical distinctions would really define or explain the deeper differences – the cohesiveness and continuity of these groups. The deeper differences are spiritual, psychical, differences – undoubtedly based on the physical, but infinitely transcending them.[124]

This became the foundation of his argument for what he called "race conservation." DuBois believed that it was necessary for the "Negro" to have the opportunity to make his contribution to the

123 Ibid.
124 Ibid., 40-42.

greater civilization. DuBois saw several obstacles standing in the way of the Negro opportunity. He suggested that as other nomadic tribes came together over time to form cities and eventually nations they were able to transcend their physical differences. As their physical differences gave way to, and were replaced by, common domicile the spiritual and psychic differences of the nations became deeper and more decisive. "When at last cities began to coalesce into nations there was another breaking down of barriers which separated groups of men. The larger and broader differences of color, hair and physical proportions were not by any means ignored, but myriads of minor differences disappeared, and the sociological and historical races of men began to approximate the present division of races as indicated by physical researches." It is at this point that the "spiritual and psychical differences of race groups which constituted the nations became deep and decisive." Here he gives specific examples:

> The English nation stood for constitutional liberty and commercial freedom; the German nation for science and philosophy; the Romance nations stood for literature and art, and the other race groups are striving, each in its own way, to develop for civilization its particular message, its particular ideal, which shall help to guide the world nearer and nearer that perfection of human life for which we all long, that "one far-off Divine event."[125]

From DuBois' point of view the Negro, as well as the yellow race, had yet to have the opportunity to make their "message" heard and contribute to human civilization. The primary obstacle standing in the way of the Negro and other people of color from getting their message out and making a contribution was the underdevelopment of their "race" as a group. At this point in his argument, DuBois makes a profound and timeless observation. He does not name

125 Ibid., 42.

slavery or Jim Crow oppression as the reason for the Negro's lack of contribution. Rather, he believed that the Negro and other people of color had to avoid being assimilated by white America. He believed that black people needed to develop their own cultural expression apart from an imitation of white culture: "For this reason," he argued, "the advance guard of the Negro people – the eight million people of Negro blood in the United States of America – must soon come to realize that if they are to take their just place in the van of Pan-Negroism, then their destiny is not absorption by the white Americans." Thus, he called for a distinctive identity devoted to "Negro ideals": "That if in America it is to be proven for the first time in the modern world that not only are Negroes capable of evolving individual men like Toussaint the Saviour, but are a nation stored with wonderful possibilities of culture, then their destiny is not a servile imitation of Anglo-Saxon culture, but a stalwart originality which shall unswervingly follow Negro ideals.[126]

As we have seen, DuBois rejected the biological argument for the maintenance of racial groups. He instead developed a strong argument for maintaining racially distinct groupings, based not primarily on biology, but on the necessity for people of color to avoid assimilation:

> It may, however, be objected here that the situation of our race in America renders this attitude impossible; that our sole hope of salvation lies in our being able to lose our race identity in the commingled blood of the nation; and that any other course would merely increase the friction of races which we call race prejudice, and against which we have so long and so earnestly fought.[127]

126 Ibid., 42-43.
127 Ibid., 43.

The question at hand, as DuBois saw it, was whether America could produce a multicultural community, a melting pot, which included blacks and other people of color, as equal partners and contributors. Could American do this without demanding that the Negro lose their racial identity in the commingled blood of the nation?

In sum, DuBois chose to ignore the battle against racialization because, in his mind, eliminating racial categories would result in the assimilation of black people by the white majority. He did offer the following critique on white America: "Here, it seems to me, is the reading of the riddle that puzzles so many of us. We are Americans, not only by birth and by citizenship, but by our political ideals, our language, our religion. Farther than that, our Americanism does not go."[128] Even if the American melting pot managed to develop common citizenship, political ideals, language and religion, it could not create an identity all inclusive enough to overcome the rules of racialization.

This chapter is the first stage in a conversation regarding the critique of racism and racialization in American society. Washington laid the groundwork in this critique with his argument for economic reforms. DuBois carried the critique further with his call for legal equality. His major contribution, the creation of the NAACP, was to have a profound effect on race relations in the twentieth century. Nonetheless, even though he countered those who argued for a scientific basis for the racial superiority of one group over another, he still sought to preserve some notion of racial identity for black people in America. He was concerned that eliminating racial categories would result in the assimilation of black people by the white majority. Thus, although he provided a powerful critique of *racism* in American society, he still accepted the main premises of *racialization*, a worldview that organizes human beings into racial groups purportedly based on biological differences.

128 Ibid.

# CHAPTER THREE

## *James H. Cone and Gayraud Wilmore*

We turn now to the second stage of this conversation about racism and racialization in American society. We turn to two major black theologians who offered in the twentieth century a profound critique of the racism in white theology: James Cone and Gayraud Wilmore. If Washington initiated the call for economic justice and DuBois carried on a deeper legal and cultural critique for racism in American society, then Cone and Wilmore called for a deeper theological critique of the racism embedded in Christian theology. In different ways, Cone and Wilmore provided a thoroughgoing examination of the deeply embedded racist assumptions in much of Christian theology and practice. In doing so, they called black Americans to a deeper recognition of their own distinctive theological voice. In different ways, they each made a case for the need for black Americans to have a deep awareness of their distinctive perspective and the ways that perspective affects how they do theology. In this, they made a very important contribution to the critique of racism in Christian theology. Nonetheless, their arguments were rooted in deeply racial categories; their arguments were rooted in articulatin
what was distinctive about an African American racial perspecti

In this chapter, I examine their arguments in order to brin
fore the ways in which their criticism of racism were, inde

in profoundly racial arguments. I will argue in later chapters for the need to move beyond an approach to theological argument that is rooted primarily in racial warrants. Nonetheless, in this chapter, I seek to bring to the fore the contributions of these theologians. Although their criticism of racism was rooted in categories that were still "racial" and thus still deeply embedded within a "racialized" standpoint, they nonetheless made an important contribution by emphasizing the need for a distinctive African American voice as an initial step in the move toward to racial justice and integration.

## JAMES H. CONE

The major emphasis of James Cone's writing has been a theological critique of white theology focused on the fact that the early church councils did not ask questions relevant to marginalized people or to poor people. "What is the significance of Nicea and Chalcedon," he asks, "for those who knew Jesus not as a thought in their heads to be analyzed in relation to a similar thought called God? They knew Jesus as a Savior and a friend, as the 'lily of the valley and the bright and morning star.'" And not only the early church councils, but even twentieth century theologians did not immediately address the concerns of black people: "What could Karl Barth possibly mean for black students who had come from the cotton fields of Arkansas, Louisiana and Mississippi, seeking to change the structure of their lives in a society that had defined black ...n being?"[129]

... Jesus spent a lot of time with the poor and ...sted that the poor and disenfranchised of ...ied to black people of the twentieth century. ... Scripture directly to black experience: "I

...*Oppressed*, rev. ed. (New York: Orbis, 1997), 5.

turn to the Jesus of Matthew, Mark, Luke, John, and Paul and of the Spirituals and Gospel Music, Fannie Lou Hamer, and Martin Luther King, Jr." The Jesus he knew directly related to contemporary black experience: "This Jesus of the biblical and black traditions is not a theological concept but a liberating presence in the lives of the poor in their fight for dignity and worth. This is the Jesus I wrote about in *God of the Oppressed*."[130] Cone contends that the Jesus that he relates to, and the Jesus that black people have related to from the beginning, was a Jesus who was present with them in the mist of their suffering and experiences of oppression. The Jesus of Luther, Calvin, and Barth was a Jesus who was based on these theological concepts and traditions developed as a result of the concepts. White theology is racist because it is written from a white point of view and does not consider the experiences of black people. For theology to be truly representative of the gospel, it must be black. Black Theology represents theology that observes the biblical text and the gospel through the black experience.

Of course, Cone does also call for a non-racialized American society. This is clear, in his earliest work entitled *Black Theology and Black Power*: "Men were not created for separation, and color is not the essence of man's humanity." Nonetheless, he goes on to observe that "we are not living in what the New Testament called the consummated Kingdom, and even its partial manifestation is not too obvious." Thus, he argues, "black people cannot live according to what ought to be, but according to what is." To be sure, human beings "ought to behave without color as the defining characteristic of their view of humanity, but they do not." Although some people can rise above racial distinctions, "existentially they live according to it, sometimes without even being conscious of it." Indeed, he contends, there are so few exceptions to this that "the universal assertion is virtually untouched." Thus, he maintains, "to ask

130 Ibid., xiii.

blacks to act as if color does not exist, to be integrated into white society, is asking them to ignore both the history of white America and present realities. Laws may be passed, but only whites have the power to enforce them."[131] It is apparent that Cone believes that the ideal society would not measure people by the color of their skin. However, like DuBois' argument, this idea is not possible because the white community has not matured to the point where it is able or willing to move beyond color. Therefore, according to Cone, blacks are forced to reckon with race and color: "Instead, in order for the oppressed blacks to regain their identity, they must affirm the very characteristic which the oppressor ridicules: blackness." Indeed, he argues, "Until white America is able to accept the beauty of blackness ('Black is beautiful, baby'), there can be no peace, no integration in the higher sense. Black people must withdraw and form their own culture, their own way of life."[132]

### *How does Cone do Theology?*

Inherent to Cone's definition of theology is the notion of God's liberating character. He makes the assumption, through his observations in the Scriptures, that the liberation character of God involves social and political implications: "Like most theologians, I believe that Christian theology is language about God. But it's more than that, and it is the 'more' that makes theology Christian. Christian theology is language about the liberating character of God's presence in Jesus Christ as he calls his people into being for freedom in the world."[133] For Cone, theology is more than a list of the communicative or non-communicative attributes about God, but

131 James H. Cone, *Black Theology and Black Power* (New York: Orbis, 1997), 17-18.
132 Ibid., 18.
133 Cone, *God of the Oppressed,* 7-8.

must also include the attribute of his character and his presence with people who have been pushed to the margins of society.

When Cone talks about liberation, he is making a distinction between the South American flavor of liberation theology and the need for liberation in the African American experience. The South American brand of liberation seems to focus on the political to the degree that it even suggests a need to overthrow government structures. Cone's perception of liberation for black Christian is not an overthrow of the government but for the social, political, cultural and ethical systems in American society to be reformed in order to produce true justice for all of its citizens.

The starting point for Cone's theology and for black theology is the black experience. He then complements this experience with what Cone calls "theological reflections." Theological reflections use the Bible as a source, but the ideas in the Bible are filtered through the primary source. Cone's primary source is his experience as a black man. In Cone's model one cannot do theology without input from the black experience. In fact, theology can be done well only from the experience of black, or at least oppressed, people. Of course, he still sees the Bible as an important source: "I still regard the Bible as an important source of my theological reflections," but he does not take the Bible as his "starting point." Instead, he contends that "the black experience and the Bible together in dialectical tension serve as my point of departure today and yesterday." For him, the order is significant: "I am black first – and everything else comes after that." This means that he reads the Bible through the lens of a "black tradition of struggle" and not as the "objective Word of God." The Bible therefore is "one witness to God's empowering presence in human affairs, along with other important testimonies."[134] In this, he shares the concerns of feminist, gay, womanist, Native American,

134 Ibid., xi-xii.

and South African black theologians, even though he does not always agree with their critical evaluation of his theological perspective. He maintains, "I have never believed that the Bible is above criticism or that it serves as an absolute judge in faith and practice."[135]

Cone also suggests that his theology starts with Jesus and that his theological reflections start with Jesus: "Turning to christology, I continue to focus on Jesus Christ as the starting point for Christian thinking about God." For Cone, Jesus Christ defines Christian identity in faith and practice. "Because I am a Christian," he asserts, "my theological reflections start with Jesus."[136]

Is this a contradiction? Cone appears to be saying that his theological reflections start with his black experience, with the Bible, and therefore Jesus, being placed in a secondary position. And yet Cone makes a clear distinction between the Scriptures themselves and the person of Jesus. The assumption here is a Barthian one: that the Bible witnesses to Jesus and is distinct from Jesus. Therefore Jesus can be the starting point and not the biblical text.

Cone contends that the Jesus that he relates to, and the Jesus that black people have related to from the beginning, was a Jesus who was present with them in the mist of their suffering and experiences of oppression. The Jesus of Luther, Calvin, and Barth was a Jesus who was based on these theological concepts and traditions that were developed as a result of the concepts. He believed that the concepts and traditions developed over the years, starting with the early church fathers, were legitimate. However, they developed their theologies or "human words about God" out of the questions that they needed to ask during their times. The questions that they were asking were not relevant questions for people who have been enslaved and have experienced white racism:

135 Ibid., xii.
136 Ibid., xiii.

Cone suggests a strong difference between a theological concept and religious-cultural and socio-political approach to understanding Jesus and doing theology. He contrasts two approaches: one that approaches Jesus as a theological concept first developed by the early church councils leading to the traditions of the reformers and another that approaches Jesus as a liberating presence of religious-cultural and socio-political significance developed in the crucible of the suffering white racism and oppression.

Cone believes that although Nicea and Chalcedon were significant, and he respects the theology that came from that period, their theology spoke to the issues of their day. However, their theology did not address questions being asked by blacks and other people of color. He respects what happened at Nicea, Chalcedon, and the theological input of the church fathers on Christology. Nonetheless, he contends that these sources are inadequate for finding out the meaning of "black folks'" Jesus. He has no difficulty with saying, "as did Athanasius that the Son is *homoousia* (one substance with the Father), especially if one has a taste for Greek philosophy and a feel for the importance of intellectual distinctions." He does not want to "minimize or detract from the significance of Athanasius' assertion for faith one iota." But, he points out, the *homoousia* question is not a black question. "Blacks do not ask whether Jesus is one with the Father or divine and human, though the orthodox formulations are implied in their language." Instead, they ask "whether Jesus is walking with them, whether they can call him up on the 'telephone of prayer' and tell him all about their troubles." To be sure Athanasius' assertion about the status of the Logos in the Godhead is important for the church's continued christological investigations. Nonetheless, he contends, we must not forget that Athanasius' question about the Son's status in relation to the Father did not arise in the historical context of the slave codes and the slave drivers: "And if he had been a black slave in America, I am sure he would have asked a different set of questions. He might have asked about the status of the Son in relation to slaveholders."

Cone raises a similar set of questions about Martin Luther and his concern about the ubiquitous presence of Jesus Christ at the Lord's Table: "While not diminishing the importance of Luther's theological concern, I am sure that if he had been born a black slave his first question would not have been whether Jesus was at the Lord's Table but whether he was really present at the slave's cabin, whether slaves could expect Jesus to be with them as they tried to survive the cotton field, the whip, and the pistol."[137]

In Cone's view, white people have interpreted the gospel according to their own interests: "Unfortunately, American theologians from Cotton Mather and Jonathan Edwards to Reinhold Niebuhr and Schubert Ogden, including radicals and conservatives, have interpreted the gospel according to the cultural and political interests of white people." White theologians have rarely attempted "to transcend the social interests of their group by seeking an analysis of the gospel in the light of the consciousness of black people struggling for liberation." Because of their "identity with the dominant power structure," they remain "largely boxed within their own cultural history."[138]

What, then, does it mean to speak the truth from a black theological perspective, that is, what are the sources and the content of theology?[139] "There is no truth for and about black people," he argues, "that does not emerge out of the context of their experience." Truth in this sense is "black truth," a truth disclosed in the history and culture of black people. This means that there can be no "Black Theology" that does not take the "black experience as a source

137 Ibid., 13.
138 Ibid., 43.
139 Cone, *God of the Oppressed*, 16.

for its starting point." According to Cone, "Black Theology is a theology of and for black people, an examination of their stories, tales, and sayings." It is an investigation of "the raw materials of our pilgrimage, telling the story of 'how we got over.'"[140] In other words, Cone suggests that theological truth only has meaning for black people when it has grown out of the experiences of black people.

*The Theologian as Preacher*

In describing the theologian's task, Cone uses terms like "the preacher," "the theologian," "the church," and their tasks almost interchangeably in the sense that they are all aiming at the same goal to emancipate the gospel from its "whiteness" so that blacks "may be capable of making an honest self-affirmation through Jesus Christ."[141] What is the church, for Cone, and what is its relationship to Christ and Black Power? "The Church is that people called into being by the power and love of God to share in his revolutionary activity for the liberation of man."[142]

In this, the church, the pastor, and the biblical scholar have the responsibility to expose the historical situation of the early church fathers. Cone is critical of Constantine's participation in the Arian controversy, which influenced not only the church's politics but also its theology and the ethical import of that theology. The reason the early church fathers could ask about the Son's relation to the Father, and later the Holy Spirit's relation to both, without connecting the question to the historical freedom of the oppressed was the historical situation in which their arguments were situated. Because the church and its bishops (during the age of Constantine and thereafter) were not slaves, "it did not occur to them that God's revelation in

140 Ibid., 16.
141 Ibid., 63.
142 Cone, *Black Theology and Black Power*, 63.

Jesus Christ is identical with the presence of his Spirit in the slave community in struggle for the liberation of humanity." According to Cone, they viewed God in "static terms" and thus tended to overlook "the political thrust of the gospel." Their theological method was consistent with "the God of Plotinus" but not with "the God of Moses and Amos." Consequently, the ethics of the fourth-century fathers differed fundamentally from biblical revelation. Instead of "standing unquestionably with the outcasts and downtrodden, as the God of the Bible does, their ethics did more to preserve the status quo than to change it."[143] Although the Fathers did ask theological questions that were presented during their time, they did not connect the theology to the ethical issues of the slave or to other ethical issue faced by the oppressed, the weak or the poor.

On the one hand, Cone argues, we must evaluate a given interpreter of Scripture in the light of the particularity of his or her history. We cannot use "the relativity of our present as the norm for the investigation of the past." Thus, we cannot criticize the early church fathers for their failure to address the critical questions of our contemporary situation. They are accountable only for dealing with "the historical issues in their time as they relate to Jesus' presence among them." On the other hand, there are "common elements in human experience that enable us to evaluate past interpreters of the faith." Because oppression of the weak by the powerful is one of those elements – and indeed, a central theme in Scripture – we can put the critical question to Athanasius, Augustine, or Luther: "What has the gospel of Jesus, as witnessed in Scripture, to do with the humiliated and the abused? If they failed to ask that question or only made it secondary in their interpretation of the gospel, then it is our task to make clear how their approach to the gospel differs from Scripture."[144]

143 Cone, *God of the Oppressed*,181.

144 Ibid., 30.

The task of the theologian is to help people understand what it is they should believe about the liberating work of God in the world. As a member of the people of God, the theologian's task is to clarify what the church believes and to do so in relation to its participation in "God's liberating work in the world." In this work, the theologian acts in the roles of "exegete, prophet, teacher, preacher, and philosopher."[145] As exegete, the theologian must find within the message the appropriate application and teach the Scripture to the human experience of those who are oppressed. Indeed, the theologian is "before all else an exegete, simultaneously of Scripture and of existence." To be an exegete of Scripture means that the theologian recognizes the Bible, the witness to God's Word, as a primary source of theological discourse. To be an exegete of existence means that Scripture is not an abstract word, not merely a rational idea, but God's Word to those who are oppressed and humiliated. The task of the theologian is to "probe the depths of Scripture exegetically for the purpose of relating that message to human existence."[146]

As prophet, the theologian takes the Word from the mouth of God to the hearts of the people. In this, the prophet also must speak prophetically to the institutions and social structures that either support or hinder the black community. As prophets they must make clear that "the gospel of God stands in judgment upon the existing order of injustice." This task involves, as Abraham Heschel said, the "exegesis of existence from a divine perspective,"[3] disclosing that "God is not indifferent to suffering and not patient with cruelty and falsehood." Indeed, God's power and judgment will continually "create justice and order out of chaos."[147]

As teachers and preachers, theologians proclaim the Word, "the truth of Jesus Christ as the Liberator of the poor and the wretched

145 Ibid., 8.
146 Ibid.
147 Ibid.

of the land." They must recognize the "passionate character" of theological language – the fact that it is always a language of "celebration and joy" because "the freedom promised is already present in the community's struggle for liberation."[148] Moreover, their sermons must always make clear that the Word and its proclamation in the black church is more than the conceptualization of theological doctrine. The Word is always more than the many "words about God." When they preach, "God's Word is a poetic happening, an evocation of an indescribable reality in the lives of the people." This, Cone maintains, is the meaning behind the occasion when a black preacher "who after reading a rather cryptic passage took off his spectacles, closed the Bible with a bang and by way of preface said, 'Brothers and sisters, this morning – I intend to explain the unexplainable find out the undefinable – ponder over the imponderable – and unscrew the inscrutable.'" In this story, the preacher is not only affirming his freedom in relation to the text; he is also making a sharp distinction between the "words of the text" and the "Word disclosed in the text."[149] He is making clear that the freedom of God to address that situation in its particularity.

### *Cone's Theology of Reconciliation*

We have been describing Cone's approach to the theological task. What lies at the heart of the content of his theology? Central to Cone's theology is a theology of reconciliation. His understanding of reconciliation, at first glance, appears to include both a vertical reconciliation with God and horizontal reconciliation with the white Christian community. He affirms that it is "a divine action that embraces the whole world, changing our relationship with God and making us new creatures." He roots all reconciliation in this divine

148 Ibid.
149 Ibid., 17.

action: "Formerly we were slaves; but reconciliation means that we are free. Formerly we were separated from God, alienated from God's will and enslaved to the evils of this world. Now we are reconciled; fellowship with God is now possible, because Christ, through his death and resurrection, has liberated us from the principalities and powers and the rulers of this present world."[150]

However, a closer look at his theology reveals that the evil separating us from God is not our personal sin but the evil principalities and powers themselves. Sin is defined as the bondage of people of color all over the world by white racist political and social systems. Atonement, then, is the reversal or neutralizing of these systems. Cone has a strong argument for the horizontal plane of reconciliation but his theology lacks an adequate understanding of the vertical relationship with God.

For Cone, reconciliation with God is found almost totally in the social, political, and economic freedom of people who have been oppressed and marginalized: "In the Bible the objective reality of reconciliation is connected with divine liberation." For him, "human fellowship with God is made possible through God's activity in history, setting people free from economic, social, and political bondage." This means that "God's act of reconciliation is not mystical communion with the divine; nor is it a pietistic state of inwardness bestowed upon the believer." Rather, God's reconciliation is "a new relationship among *people* created by God's concrete involvement in the political affairs of the world, taking sides with the weak and the helpless."[151] Cone's theology of reconciliation insists that reconciliation with God has an objective reality. In other words, he argues that there should be a corresponding ethic consistent with the theological proposition.

---

150 Ibid., 209.
151 Ibid.

Moreover, for Cone, social and political categories not only determine his definition for reconciliation, but these categories also define his definitions for justification and sanctification:

> Reconciliation is not only justification, God's righteous deliverance of slaves from bondage; it is sanctification, the slaves' acceptance of their new way of life, their refusal to define existence in any other way than in freedom. Reconciliation is not simply freedom from oppression and slavery; it is also freedom for God. That is why Paul says: "For freedom Christ has set us free."[152]

Justification is the oppressed man's deliverance from that oppression. Sanctification is man coming to terms with this new freedom, refusing to submit himself back into the former bondage. Only after oppressed people experience reconciliation, justification, and sanctification will they really experience freedom.

These ideas reveal two more important points in Cone's theology. What is Cone's understanding of God's ultimate intention for humanity? How does James Cone define freedom? Cone's understanding of God's teleological intent and his definition of freedom are two important theological concepts important for understanding his overall theology. The title for Chapter 7 of his book, *God of the Oppressed*, is "The Meaning of Liberation." Here Cone says:

> There is no liberation independent of Jesus' past, present, and future coming. He is the ground of our present freedom to struggle and the source of our hope that the vision disclosed in our historical fight against oppression will be fully realized in God's future. In this sense, liberation is not a human possession but a divine gift of freedom to those who struggle in faith against violence and oppression. Liberation

152 Ibid., 213.

> is not an object but the project of freedom wherein the oppressed realize that their fight for freedom is a divine right of creation.[153]

Liberation is Jesus Christ and it is the freedom to struggle to be free from present oppression. Freedom is the task of liberation. Liberation or freedom is the end purpose of God for a people who are struggling in an oppressed social structure: "The grounding of liberation in God's act in Jesus Christ is the logical consequence of any Christian theology that takes Scripture seriously as an important source for the doing of theology." For Cone, human freedom in Scripture is about "hope for a new heaven and a new earth is grounded in God's freedom." In this view, divine freedom is not merely "an affirmation of the self-existence and complete transcendence of God over creaturely existence." Rather, it also expresses "God's will to be in relation to creatures in the social context of their striving for the fulfillment of humanity." That is, "God is free to be for us."[154]

Cone talks about freedom for God as well as freedom for the oppressed. Freedom for God is to be in a relationship with a people free of oppression. It seems then, for Cone, liberation or freedom from oppression is the intended end for God and his people. One problem with Cone's insistence on framing his theology within the matrix of a racialized worldview and locating freedom and liberation from the sin of individual and institutional human oppression is that it negates the gospel's atoning efficacy for those who are not experiencing these types of oppression other than their participation as the oppressor. Under these circumstances reconciliation will be impossible.

153 Ibid., 127.
154 Ibid., 128.

*Black Power and Black Theology*

Cone's theology of reconciliation, with its focus on freedom has important implications for his understanding of "black power." Indeed, the theme of "black power" is central to Cone's theology. What does Cone mean by black power? Cone offers a series of quotes all giving a descriptive definition of black power. First, the phrase black power advocates "emancipation." It means "complete emancipation of black people from white oppression by whatever means black people deem necessary." Its methods may "include selective buying, boycotting, marching, or even rebellion." But whatever form it takes, black power means "black freedom, black self-determination, wherein black people no longer view themselves as without human dignity but as men, human beings with the ability to carve out their own destiny." In short, and here Cone quotes Stokely Carmichael, "Black Power means T.C.B., Take Care of Business – black folk taking care of black folks' business, not on the terms of the oppressor, but on those of the oppressed."[155] Secondly, black power is determined to stop oppression. Black power asserts that "oppression can be endured no longer in the style that the oppressor takes for granted." To assert black power is "say No" and to reject categorically "the humiliating orders of the master." By so doing, black power affirms that something that is placed above everything else, including life itself. To say "No" means to assert that death is preferable to life, if the latter is devoid of freedom: "Better to die on one's feet than to live on one's knees."[156] Thirdly, black power is determined not to wait any longer for justice. With black power, the black man prefers to die than surrender to some other value. With black power, the black man does not accept "the white society's appeal to wait or to be orderly." To do so would be to affirm "something which is less than essential being."[157] Fourth,

155 Ibid., 6
156 Ibid.
157 Ibid., 7.

black power affirms black dignity. It is, in short, "an attitude, an inward affirmation of the essential worth of blackness." With black power, the black man will not "be poisoned by the stereotypes that others have of him, but will affirm from the depth of his soul: 'Get used to me, I am not getting used to anyone.'"[158] Finally, black power is the power of the black man to say "Yes" to his own "black being," and "to make the other accept him or be prepared for a struggle."[159]

Thus, Cone interprets this understanding of black power in explicitly theological terms. If a black person is truly to respond to God's love in faith, then they must accept as truth "the new image of himself revealed in Jesus Christ." Because of this, he now knows "that the definition of himself defined by white society is inconsistent with the newly found image disclosed in Christ." Because of his identity in Christ, the new black person can affirm who he or she is as a black person. In a world that has taught blacks to hate themselves, he need not "transcend" his blackness. Rather, he can accept it and love it as a gift of the Creator. He knows that until he accepts himself "as a being of God in all of its physical blackness, he can love neither God nor neighbor." Indeed, Cone avers, "this may be what one Black Power advocate meant when he said: 'Until blacks develop themselves, they can do nothing for humanity.' And another who said, 'Black Power does not teach hatred; it teaches love. But it teaches us that love, like charity, must begin at home; that it must begin with ourselves, our beautiful black selves.'"[160] Black power then is a state of being free, for black people, from white oppression, to self-determination, through self-proclamation. It is accomplished through blacks standing their ground for freedom.

158 Ibid., 8.
159 Ibid.
160 Ibid., 52-53.

## GAYRAUD WILMORE

Like Cone, Wilmore is another mid-twentieth century African American theologian who sought to offer a critique of white Christian theology in light of the African American experience. Although his style was not as polemical as Cone's, he also sought to help black Americans become more aware of the distinctiveness of their experience within American and how that distinctive perspective offered a different way of construing the theological task.

Wilmore served as a pastor and a theologian but his greatest contributions came in his role as a church historian. He documented the history of Black Religion and served on several black church councils during and after the civil rights movements of the 1950s, 1960s, and 1970s. On the one hand, he insisted that "racial identity should be no bar to full fellowship and participation in the church and in society."[161] Wilmore believes that an integrated society and church is possible. However, in order for this integration to take place, white Christians need to acquire an appreciation for the particular experience of black humanity in America. This experience has, in many cases, created a sensibility and perception rarely identical with those born white in America. These perceptions and sensibilities often lead "to a certain depth and richness, a certain passion for justice that can discern in the truth about Jesus Christ that which modern White Christians have both forgotten and ignored."[162] So, the white Christian needs to come to an appreciation of the contribution that people of color can make to their own white Christian experience. However, these perceptions and sensibilities come with a price that leaves people of color with the responsibility to rise above the denigrating effects on their own sense of self.

Wilmore is especially critical of the way liberal theologians in

161 Gayraud S. Wilmore and James H. Cone, eds., *Black Theology: A Documentary History, 1966-1979* (Maryknoll, NY: Orbis, 1979), 95.
162 Ibid., 95.

the United States "never calculated the extent to which the infusion of God's love for others is related to the freedom and ability to affirm and esteem oneself." In his view, they neglected to state the extent to which "the achievement of authentic personhood" (which, he argues, is a "prerequisite of discipleship") is related to the need for "a positive sense of historic community and group experience." Thus, central to his theology is the claim that "self-esteem based on group identity precedes and supersedes, at least for people who have known segregation, a satisfactory experience of *koinonia* in most interracial churches."[163] Thus, for Wilmore, integration means to proceed beyond the superficial. Blacks and other people of color need to be empowered to have a healthy sense of their own racial identity as a subculture within the macro white culture.

### *How does Wilmore do Theology?*

Wilmore presents a sophisticated and nuanced argument for integration. On the one hand, he insists that "racial identity should be no bar to full fellowship and participation in the church and in society."[164] At first he appears to be supporting an integrated Christian society. On the other hand, Wilmore is critical of those who suggest that "brotherly love, social programs and the unity of mankind in the family of God required the disappearance of all ethnic and racial identity and separateness." He is critical of those who think that "the closure of sociological and spiritual space between the races would bring about 'nonsegregated churches and a nonsegregated society.' In such a church and society, all black cats would appear to be gray."[165]

Thus, although Wilmore believes that an integrated society and

163 Ibid.
164 Ibid.
165 Ibid.

church is possible, he also argues that in order for this integration to take place white Christians need to acquire an appreciation for the particular experience of black humanity in America. This experience has, in many cases, created a sensibility and perception rarely identical with those who born white in America. These perceptions and sensibilities often lead "to a certain depth and richness, a certain passion for justice that can discern in the truth about Jesus Christ, that which modern White Christians have both forgotten and ignored."[166] So, the white Christian needs to come to an appreciation of the contribution that people of color can make to their own Christian experience.

In addition to describing what whites need to do in order to appreciate blacks more fully, Wilmore also places responsibility at the feet of black Americans. He acknowledges that the sensibilities and perceptions come to people of color in a context of a "matrix of psychological and physical suffering, segregation, discrimination and the every-present remembrance of a previous condition of involuntary servitude."[167] However, he also contends that these perceptions and sensibilities come with a price, which leaves people of color with the responsibility to rise above the denigrating effects on their own sense of self. Thus, he argues that for meaningful integration to proceed beyond the superficial, blacks and other people of color are going to need to be empowered to have a healthy sense of their own racial identity as a subculture within the macro white culture.

Given his stress on the need for a healthy sense of self, Wilmore speaks of both individual and corporate transformation. Although, like Cone, his stress is on the need for social and political transformation, he also speaks of "divine presence" within the "solitude and

166 Ibid.
167 Ibid.

inwardness of individuals." What he emphasizes is that "what we can say about a God whose divine presence is in the solitude and inwardness of individuals cannot be separated from our knowledge of his action in the structures of society and the politics of nations." In his view, when we speak of "God the Father of Jesus Christ as the God of men and nations" we cannot separate the "inwardness of faith" from its "outwardness." He argues that "the man of faith" knows God's presence "at both levels of experience." Moreover, he knows that "they so impinge upon and interpenetrate each other as to become one." The man of faith "cannot speak of the inwardness of faith without speaking at the same time of its outwardness." He cannot separate "the sacred and the secular, the authority of structures in human life from the authority of spirit, the works of love from the works of justice." In other words, he cannot, in any ultimate sense, "disengage the salvation of individuals from the creation of the world and cosmic redemption through Jesus Christ."[168] In sum, for Wilmore, the message and the power of the gospel should transform not only individuals but also societies exposed to the gospel message. It has both inward and outward authority.

These profound interconnections lie at the heart of Wilmore's theology. Although he has more of a place for the individual experience of faith than Cone, Wilmore also lays stress on God's activity within political and social structures. He is also critical of highly abstract formulations of theology that are divorced from people's daily experience. In his description of the theological task, he acknowledges that the word theology comes from two Greek words – *theos* ("God") and *logos* ("word" or "thought"). He affirms that theology is "simply words about God or thinking about God." But for many Christians, he observes, "theology is remote, abstract, baffling, confusing, and boring." Because of this,

168 Gayraud S. Wilmore, *The Secular Relevance of the Church* (Philadelphia: Westminster Press, 1963), 18-19.

"they turn it over to the professionals – the theologians – who can ponder and inquire into the ways of God with the world."[169] By contrast, he seeks to approaches theology, the Scriptures, and God by asking a fundamental question about the church's social strategies in terms of its definition and commitment to the mission of social change. In his introduction to one of his major books, *The Secular Relevance of the Church*, he presents a question that lies at the heart of much of his work: "Can the church of Christ, as represented in this discussion by the Protestant churches, become an effective influence for basic change and reconstruction in a highly technological, secularized society?[170]

Wilmore believes that the majority of Protestant churches are out of touch with a meaningful strategy for social action and mission. Yet, at the same time, he does not reject the validity of their emphasis. It just is not sufficient to address the real needs of society. "Protestant churches," he observes, "continue to understand the nature and mission of the church in terms of preaching Sunday sermons, saving souls, and inculcating the moral standards of a traditionalistic and rural society." As a result of strictly focusing on these activities, there is among most Protestant churches, in his view, "a studied avoidance of the role of organizing institutional power and a commitment to social action as a basic strategy of mission."[171] Wilmore believes that this emphasis is leading the church to continue to ask old questions which are valid but have already been answered. He has no difficulty with the classical questions of western Christian theology: "The argument we will present does not have to do with whether or not individual persons are of ultimate concern to God and should be the object of the mission of the church. That question has already been answered. The Bible and almost two thousand years of

169 Gayraud S. Wilmore, *Last Things First (Library of Living Faith)* (Philadelphia: Westminster Press, 1982), 7.
170 Wilmore, *The Secular Relevance of the Church,* 3.
171 Ibid., 4.

church history and theology have answered it affirmatively." Thus, he has no sound reason for discarding that answer even though, he acknowledges, in attempting to discover what it means today, "we may seem to be denying its validity." As we have acknowledged, Wilmore has no difficulty with the individual expressions of faith. Nonetheless, the thrust of his concern is with "whether a religion that speaks only about love, humility, sobriety, personal integrity, honesty, and other individualistic virtues has any real possibility of changing the world in which we live."[172] In raising this concern, he is not arguing that "the Church of Christ should try to dominate secular society, whether it can today undertake political action as a full-blown political party, or erect a new 'Christian economic system' to replace present systems." His question, rather, is whether the honorable virtues associated with personal transformation "have any possibility of relevant meaning or of realization in a rationalized, technological society unless the churches recover a comprehensive cultural vocation that has a great deal more to say than this, and is able to speak through social and political action."[173]

At the heart, then, of his theology is the attempt to "recover a comprehensive cultural vocation" and can "speak through social and political action."[174] But to do this, the church must cultivate new theological and ethical formulations. Old formulations do not provide the theological basis for an ethical analysis and criticism of social problems; they do not help people to evaluate customary forms of community life and values; and they do not provide an adequate theological-ethical basis for relating the scientific study of social institutions to the development of Christian social policy.[175]

172 Ibid., 4-5.
173 Ibid., 4-5.
174 Ibid., 5.
175 Ibid.

*The Kingdom of God*

In this task, recovering a focus on the kingdom of God is central to Wilmore's work. For Wilmore, the kingdom is the realm in which God's reign is realized. He suggests it is significant that in the prayer that we have learned from Jesus the first petition is that the kingdom, or reign, of God should become present and effective in the world.[176] The kingdom is present but not completed realized; it is invisible, yet it is the visible church which is ruled over by Christ. We speak, therefore, of the presence of the kingdom, but at the same time of its coming in the future. Because it is not yet here, we hope for it, but to hope for it means that in some sense we are already living under its power, which impels us to "make it real": "If the coming of the Kingdom is the first thing that Christians should pray for, it is a reasonable conclusion that it also occupies the highest priority in what we should hope for. But that is not all. Our hope seems uniquely realistic, because in some sense the Kingdom has already begun."[177]

Wilmore's understanding of the kingdom includes both the Lordship of Jesus and the entrance into of an exceptional relationship with each other as brothers and sisters in Christ: "Jesus understood himself fully in relation to this new situation. He was anointed by the Spirit of God to proclaim the fulfillment of the time of preparation and the opening of the door of God's favor for those who were ready to accept his Lordship and enter into an exceptional relationship with him and with one another."[178] What does Wilmore mean by the phrase "an exceptional relationship with one another?" He means here that the kingdom, although it is a spiritual kingdom, is not limited to the non-physical. The kingdom, and therefore the reign of God through His church body, would include addressing the poor the sick and marginalized members both inside and outside of

176 Wilmore, *Last Things First*, 54.
177 Ibid., 54.
178 Ibid.

the covenant community. This understanding is manifest in Jesus' ministry on earth explained to his disciples. Jesus said that the evidence of this new kingdom was the healing of the sick and in the message of good news to the poor. The signs of this new state of affairs were evident. It was not something that people had to conjure up in their imaginations or think themselves into. It was not "accentuating the positive and eliminating the negative." The empirical evidence of the kingdom was plain for all to see. When John's disciples asked Jesus if he was the promised Messiah who would bring in the kingdom, Jesus said, "Go and tell John what you hear and see: the blind receive their sight and the lame walk, the lepers are cleansed and the deaf hear, and the dead are raised up, and the poor have good news preached to them. And blessed is he who takes no offense at me" (Matt. 11:4-6).

How does he understand salvation and the Lordship of Christ? For Wilmore, the Lordship of Christ is understood in relation to the "divine presence" in both "the solitude and inwardness of individuals" and the "knowledge of his action in the structures of society and the politics of nations." Indeed, he argues that history is the context in which Christ has to do with us as individuals because we look at history from the point of view of faith in the Lordship of Christ. From this point of view, history has cosmic dimensions. On the one hand, it concerns "the here and now, the concrete and time-bound." At the same time, it encompasses "all time and space and has its beginning and end, its purpose and meaning, in a reality that is beyond itself." This, then, is what Wilmore means when he speaks of "the God and Father of Jesus Christ as the God of men and nations."[179]

One of the distinctive features in Wilmore's understanding of the kingdom of God is his understanding of the relationship between the church and the world. He uses several terms to identify this

179 Wilmore, *The Secular Relevance of the Church*, 18-19.

relationship. The main two terms are "Spurious Secularism" and "True Secularity." "Spurious Secularism" would be characterized by those pastors who take their lead from the culture and not the Lord. Their ministry is no different from the Rotary Club or the Kiwanis Club. Not working in tune with the gospel or the true mission of the church, they are middle-classed religious people who do not get anything done beyond putting limitations on dancing, smoking, or playing cards. Wilmore says that these people can be politically and theologically conservative. Wilmore also included in this category those who hold to a personal salvation and individualistic morality although their theology does not produce a social ethic.

Nonetheless, although he speaks "critically, sometimes harshly, of the old theological-ethical emphasis upon a gospel of personal salvation and an individualistic morality better suited for a rural culture than for the megalopolis of today," he does not mean to repudiate "the person-centered elements in the New Testament and in Christian faith and life." Rather, he argues that we must find theological formulations that are most relevant today – formulations that are "no less Biblical," but which develop these themes in a new context. Thus, far from "dropping out of the Christian faith a concern for the individual," he argues that we must locate "the individual" and minister to his needs "in his real situation before God and his brother."[180] Thus, he believes that there is a way to have a proactive social agenda without compromising biblical integrity. This, then, is what he means by a "true secularity." How do we enact "the true secularity" of the church? We do so by "believing and acting out realistically the message that Jesus Christ is not only the Lord of the church but is also the Lord of General Motors and the Democratic Party and is working quite outside the church as such, to fulfill the reconciliation of the world."[181]

180 Ibid., 17.
181 Ibid., 21.

### *Africentrism*

A central concept in Wilmore's theology is the theme of Africentrism. Wilmore describes his work as Africentric because it results from "looking at the world I know as an African American Christian and being open to angles of vision that differ from Euro-American interpretations of history and ways of understanding the Christian faith." His work is informed and inspired by his personal experience as a member "of the African diaspora of the Christian church, and because they look toward Africa and the diaspora, rather than toward the North Atlantic community, for authentication and authority."[182]

Wilmore admits that it is difficult to find a precise definition of "Africentric lens." Molefi Kete Asante, Cain Hope Felder and J. Deotis Roberts – other thinkers who have used this term – each define the idea a little differently. Wilmore uses the term Africentrism to describe a way of viewing the world through an African American or, in his words, Africentric lens. An Africentric lens is a way of seeing the world and a commitment to Christianity that overcomes the historic oppression experienced by African-Americans in general. This lens allows and enables blacks to empower themselves with an unhindered sense of reality. As he uses this term, Africentrism "involves doing intellectual work with Africans and African Americans – with their histories, their cultures, and their peoples – as one reflects on human affairs and what is transpiring in the world." He argues that "Africentrism is the lens some people use to correct a distorted vision of reality that we inherited either by seduction or imposition." Thinking through an Africentric lens involves "centering the picture of the world that we have in our minds – namely, our worldview – so that our actions, our functional deportment, our modus vivendi will support the historic struggle of

182 Ibid., 10.

Africans and the African diaspora for freedom, justice, and equality in a world that has been colonized, dominated, and interpreted by white Europeans and Americans to the disadvantage and detriment of most people of color." In other words, Africentrism presents a way of viewing reality other than from a Eurocentric outlook. Moreover, it entails "a serious attempt to understand the manner in which Africans have viewed reality in their context of culture for thousands of years before they encountered the Western worldview." Through the lens of Africentrism, African Americans can seek "to recover their classical roots through empathy, knowledge, and experience." Through these "new looking glasses," they can "peer into this Africentered world to observe what may be useful in our commitment to Christianity." In doing so, they can ask: What is useful? What must be rejected? What will enrich and empower our Christian way of life?[183]

Wilmore recognizes that "putting African and African American lenses into the spectacles with which people view the faith and the world will help those people, whose eyes (and souls) were otherwise out of focus, to see and respond to voluminous data and phenomena from "an alternative perspective" that is beneficial not only for black people but for everyone!"[184] The term Africentrism implies is "a way of viewing reality other than from a Eurocentric outlook."[185] An Africentric lens, therefore, entails a critique of a "Eurocentric" lens for viewing reality. If, indeed, a Eurocentric lens is the default lens being used by almost everyone, then an Africentric lens offers a critique of that perspective. An Africentric lens implies that Christians of European descent and other Christians who look at Christianity through the European lens must also recognize the existence and limitations of their perspective.

183 Gayraud S. Wilmore, *Pragmatic Spirituality: The Christian Faith through an Africentric Lens* (New York: University Press, 2004), 8.
184 Wilmore, *Pragmatic Spirituality,* 9-10.
185 Ibid., 10.

Of course, the difficulty with using this distinction between an Africentric and a Eurocentric lens is that these two ways of viewing reality are still defined in relation to each other. An Africentric lens still is defined in relation to a Eurocentric, which serves as the measure against which it is defined. And here we arrive at the limits of talk about an Africentric and a Eurocentric perspective. If either lens is used as the standard for measuring the other, then there is no criterion beyond either stance for making an evaluation. Nonetheless, the constructive contribution of Wilmore's Africentric lens model is that his work, and the work of other black theologians, is validating experience of black Christians. Their work is also empowering the black Christians, giving them a voice with which to come to the table of dialogue. The next step for Christians, who bring both the Africentric lens and the Eurocentric lens, is to come around the table of dialogue and together discover an authentic Christianity that addresses both groups as human beings.

## A CRITIQUE OF BLACK THEOLOGY

Both Cone and Wilmore have made important contributions to the development of black theology in the mid-twentieth theology. They both sought to identify what was distinctive to the experience of black Americans and from that basis articulate a critique of white theology (in Cone's terms) or Eurocentric theology (in Wilmore's terms). In doing so, they both sought to emphasize the ways Christian theology offers resources that empower black Americans to articulate a distinctive theology that expresses how they experience God's transformative work in their lives and in society at large. In different ways, they each have made an important contribution to the theological critique of racism in American society. They each have provided a theological framework for articulating what black Americans have experienced and for criticizing the larger social and political patterns that have diminished their sense of dignity in American life.

Nonetheless, there are limitations to their approach. Cheryl Sanders has provided an interesting and powerful critique of the Black Theology movement in the twentieth that sheds light some of the limitations of their approach. On the one hand, she argues that Black Theology cannot offer strategies for African American men and women who have already experienced liberation: "What sources of ethical guidance are available," she asks, "for those individuals and groups who have made the transition from victimization to moral agency, that is, for those who are already experiencing liberation?" How does this theology "shed light upon the moral challenges faced by African American men and women who are in charge of their own institutions and resources, given that the liberatory discourse has primarily been pursued by and among persons who are comfortably ensconced within the elite academic structures of the dominant culture?" How does this theology encourage such persons "retain a strong sense of identity and level of engagement with those who have not yet experienced liberation?"[186]

On the other hand, she observes that although black liberation theology offers a starting place for dialogue on race relations, the discussion and practical implications of the movement has not reached the rank-and-file African American churches, to say nothing about the millions of African American Christians whose lives have been totally unaffected by the movement. Referring to C. Eric Lincoln's and Lawrence H. Mamiya's landmark study (in 1990) of black churches, she points out that the black liberation theology has largely been an intellectual movement occurring largely among the educated elite of the black clergy that has had a limited impact upon

186 Cheryl J. Sanders, *Empowerment Ethics for a Liberated People: A Path to African American Social Transformation* (Minneapolis, MN, Fortress Press: 1995), 1.

the black churches. Indeed, she avers, "the great majority of black urban ministers in the United States at least two-thirds of them have not been affected by the movement at all."[187] In this, her criticism of the black theology movement echoes Cone's own critique of patristic and reformation theological movement. Like these earlier theological movements, the black theology movement is also limited to issues experienced by the elite.

Moreover, in her view, because Black Theology continues to work within the very categories that presuppose that whites are the oppressors and blacks are the victims, it does not provide "the constructive ethical task of delineating steps to be taken by the oppressed to ensure that the experience of empowerment does not result in assimilation of the most dehumanizing values and behaviors of the oppressing group, and in reduplication of intra-group oppression."[188] For Sanders, black theology does not provide the means for engaging in a deeper critique of the very ways in which an oppressing group perpetuates dehumanizing values and behaviors so that intra-group oppression is not reduplicated. Indeed, she argues, "meaningful moral progress toward justice can be derived neither from the internalization of the oppressor's values nor from the insistence that one's own liberation is always someone else's obligation."[189] What resources does black theology provide for the deeper critique of the internalization of the oppressors values? What resources does black theology provide for assuming responsibility for one's own liberation?

Finally, Sanders draws attention to the idea that the church should be able to minister across race, sex, and class lines – that it should not solely be identified with the concerns of one particular racial group. In general, she argues, the Christian faith provides a

187 Ibid., 2.
188 Ibid.
189 Ibid.

clear rationale for establishing ministering relationships across the lines of sex, race, and class: "Christians of all races can be found doing the work of ministry, propelled to enact, and not merely to quote, the foundational Gospel text for prophetic engagement in the name of Christ (Luke 4:18)."[190] Sanders believes that Christianity presents an argument for multicultural community and, in her view, the black liberation theology does not offer models to help the church achieve that end.

Sanders' critique brings us to the limits of Cone's and Wilmore's arguments. By emphasizing the distinctive contributions a black or Africentric perspective makes to the theological task, Cone and Wilmore have created a space for black Americans to claim a distinctive angle on the theological task, an angle that enables them both to name and articulate their own experience of oppression as blacks and provide a critique of the ways white theology is either irrelevant to that experience or continues to reinforce that oppression. Nonetheless, there are limits inherent in their approaches, limits that are inherent in the very fact that they have sought to articulate a theology defined primarily by their experience as African Americans. Indeed, we might observe, the very standpoint on which their critique is defined is a standpoint inherently defined by their relationship as blacks to whites, and thus is inherently defined by racial distinctions. With this critique in mind, we turn next to another theologian, J. Deotis Roberts, who sought to address not only the problem of racism but also the problem of articulating a theology defined primarily in terms of racial categories.

190 Ibid.

# CHAPTER FOUR

## *J. Deotis Roberts and White Evangelicals*

In this chapter, we turn to a third theologian who contributed to the black theology movement of the sixties and seventies. Of the three theologians we examine in this study, J. Deotis Roberts is the most conservative in his standpoint on the authority of the Scripture and in his overall understanding of Christian theology. Moreover, his argument for a move beyond "liberation" to one of "reconciliation" makes his position more compatible with that of John Perkins, whom we will discuss in the next chapter.

At the heart of Roberts' proposal for "black theology" is a critique of the cultural presuppositions of white theology. He argues that white theologians are embedded in a European and Greek worldview that influences their interpretation of Scripture. In the same way that black Americans need to become aware of how their cultural context influences their reading of Scripture, so white Americans need to become aware that they too do not approach Scripture from culturally neutral standpoint. As Roberts avers, "it is more honest to admit our particularities."[191] It is precisely by admitting our particularities, he argues, that we can best come to a

191 J. Deotis Roberts, "Contextual Theology: Liberation and Indigenization," *ChickenBones: A Journal for Literary and Artistic African American Themes*, http://nathanielturner.com/contextualtheology.htm (accessed August 24, 2008).

more nearly "universal" understanding of the gospel's import for all people. With a focus on a universal understanding of the gospel's import – and the implications this universal understanding has for his understanding of "reconciliation" – Roberts' theology has a slight shift of emphasis from that of Cone and Wilmore. In this chapter, we examine how his proposal for a black theology both brings to the fore the particularities in black and white approaches to theological reflection even as it seeks to move toward a more universal understanding of the Gospel's import, one which has implications not only for the liberation of blacks, but also for moving toward reconciliation with whites.

## THE AUTHORITY OF SCRIPTURE AND THE INCARNATION

Although he does not take the verbal plenary inspiration of Scripture view of many conservative evangelicals, he does have a high view of Scripture more in line with conservative evangelicals than the others in the study. For him, the Bible is "the most important source of our knowledge of God." It is "the Word of God, regardless of the limitations of the human words through which it comes to us." It is "the living Word of God insofar as it bears witness to God's revealing the divine mind and will to us in Jesus Christ."[192] Because of his views on Scripture, Roberts can more easily enter dialogue with conservative evangelicals and many mainline Protestants as well as Catholics.

Not only Roberts' position on Scripture, but his position on the person and work of Jesus are also positions consistent with conservative evangelicals. Roberts takes the position that the mission of God, the ministry of Jesus, and the mission of the church are inter-

---

192 J. Deotis Roberts, *Christian Beliefs*, 3rd ed. (Silver Spring, MD: The J. Deotis Roberts Press, 2000), 1-7.

consistent and directly connected to the incarnation of Jesus. For Roberts, "the coming of Christ has a special meaning in theology." He relates Christ's coming to the "incarnation," Christ's "embodiment or enfleshment." God enters history in Jesus Christ: "Through the coming of Christ, God confronts us where we live our lives. We are at the center of our faith as we discuss the "Word made flesh.""[193]

Roberts relates the incarnation of Jesus to the mission of the church. He says that the ministry of the church is incarnational, meaning that the way the church functions in the world, outside of the four walls, is to make Jesus living and present in the lives of people carrying out what God wants done in the earth. Thus, the church that Jesus founded is "an extension of the incarnation." For Christians, Jesus is "God's supreme salvific revelation to humans through fleshly and historical embodiment." The church, in turn, is the means "by which that revelation is manifest in community and throughout history." The church, therefore, becomes important as the context of ministry. It is through the church's mission and ministry that "God's will is to be done on earth."[194]

What kind of ministry is the church to enact, if it is to act out of the power of Jesus' ministry? Jesus' ministry was "holistic" in that it looked at the entire person. His concern went farther than saving the souls of his followers. He was also concerned about their physical lives. Jesus' ministry was also holistic in that he addressed the systemic issues that people faced every day.[195]

Roberts talks about the ministry of Jesus being three-fold: it was priestly, prophetic, and public. First, Jesus' ministry was priestly. The role of a priest is to provide comfort and assurance to those who are suffering or in trouble. It has to do more with the compassion

193 Ibid., 64-65.

194 J. Deotis Roberts, *The Prophethood of Black Believers: An African American Political Theology for Ministry* (Louisville, KY: Westminster/John Knox Press, 1994), 1.

195 Ibid., 1.

and concern Jesus had for those whose life he touched. Jesus often "had compassion" (Mark 6:34) as he saw people who were hungry, anxious, or sick. One active area of ministry in which Jesus demonstrated this priestly aspect was healing. There was a sense that each and every person, regardless of sex, race, or class, was equally valuable in his presence. Second, Jesus' ministry was prophetic. One of the great theological insights of Dr. Martin Luther King Jr. was to see an unbroken line between the Old Testament prophets of social justice and the ministry of Jesus.[3] Jesus was not only a priest. He was also a prophet. Theologically, Jesus was obsessed with the "righteousness of God." This has to do with the ethical attributes of God. Jesus came preaching that the kingdom of God is at hand (Mark 1:15). The kingdom of which he spoke is equivalent to the "will of God." Thus, to "seek the kingdom" is to seek righteousness (Matt. 6:33). Finally, Jesus' ministry was public. Public here refers to the manner in which Jesus engaged the evils inherent in the systems of power in his time and place. Thus, the ministry of Jesus provides a basis for ministry in the public sphere.[196] Although Roberts has a lot to say about the social political issues connected to the gospel, he also believes that Christians have a pietistic responsibility in their relationship to the Godhead.

## CONTEXTUAL AND LIBERATION THEOLOGY

Given his attention to an incarnational understanding of the ministry of Jesus, Roberts was especially concerned with developing a "contextual theology." His intent in developing such a contextual theology, however, was to admit the distinctive perspectives we all bring to Scripture so that we can better understand the universal import of the Gospel for our particular situations. He sought to show how the theologies of whites in Europe and North America were

196 Roberts, *The Prophethood of Black Believers,* 2-4.

also biased by particular cultural standpoints. Roberts points out that the colonizers, Germany, Britain, and the United States, who are basically white Christians with a European and Greek worldview, come to the table with preset assumptions: "They are based upon the assumption of a social Darwinism that places Western man – his thought, religion, and culture – at the pivot. For the most part these programs aim at logical precision more than they do at ethical decision and social change."[197] These worldviews, in his view, are also driven by assumptions drawn from Greek philosophy (Aristotelian logic and Platonic dualism), assumptions that do not exhaust the thought-structures of the human race. In Roberts' view, "It is arrogant for persons who have been exposed only to these categories of thought and their derivatives to speak (*ex cathedra*) for all Christians. It is more honest to admit our particularities."[198]

In developing his own black theology, Roberts seeks to develop a theology of liberation that is resonant with other theologies of liberation that are emerging throughout the world. He observes, "If theology is to be more than dry bones for faith, if it is to address human beings of flesh and blood, if it is to deal with the ultimate issues of life and death, it must be more than a logical statement of doctrine – though it should be that." Indeed, he argues, "theology cannot be truly universal if it refuses to deal with the particularities of the human situation. It must not, however, rest with the particular.[199] The goal, then, of contextual theology is to "decolonize" theology, making it more amenable for all people around the world. In particular, Roberts is thinking about African and Asian Christians who have contributed to theological discourse. He seeks to bring to the fore those regions of the world that have largely being overlooked by Europeans and North Americans. He situates his work as a black

197 Ibid., 29-30.
198 Roberts, "Contextual Theology," 1-3.
199 Ibid., 1-3.

theologian among the work other Christian theologians are doing who are "attempting to decolonize theology and make it speak more meaningfully out of the culture and the history of the people for whom the faith is interpreted." This, in his view, is a "vital process" if theology is to be more than "dry bones" for faith. The masses of people in these parts of the world are among the "wretched of the earth" and their perspectives need to be included in Christian theological reflection.[200] Roberts believes that Black Theology can go a long way in helping this decolonization process because it too presents a different standpoint on the ways white Europeans and North Americans have approaches the theological task.

"Indigenization" is another term that Roberts uses in developing his contextual theology. Here he draws on Raymond Panikkar, a Hindu-Catholic. "He argues that Hindu philosophy should find its place in Christian thought in the same way that Plato and Aristotle found their place in Christian theology." Panikkar bases his argument on the idea that Hindu philosophy is more in line with Christianity that Aristotelian philosophy. Roberts' bottom line is not so much that we should all accept Hindu philosophy at face value but that there are new questions that should be asked of the Scriptures that were never asked before.

Roberts also locates his work as a black theologian in relation to Latin American liberation theology, which he describes as "a theology that liberates." Although Latin American liberation theology emerges out of a different context than a black theology of liberation, it has much to contribute to black theology. Both types of theology emerge out of a common experience of oppression: "It is at this point that black theologians and their African brothers in southern Africa join the oppressed in Latin America as those who belong to a fellowship that bears the mark of pain." What both theologies seek is the "the

200 J. Deotis Roberts, *A Black Political Theology* (Philadelphia: Westminster Press, 1974.), 33.

humanization of life." Both theologies argue for this humanization of life from the context of their experience as "a long-suffering people." They are bringing to the fore a "new consciousness" for understanding the gospel, a consciousness that calls for a "radical change in oppressive social attitudes and structures of power.[201]

Overall, Roberts wants theology to go beyond merely the "systematic," which often tends only deal with the realm of ideas. This type of theological reflection alone is not adequate to liberate people. It must also be empowered. He argues that there can be "no universal revelation which separates salvation history from political history." Thus, he contends that "systematic theology must become theological ethics." It cannot simply speak from "ivory towers, but from the marketplace." For theology to be worthy of the name, it must now address "nonpersons" as well as "nonbelievers."[202]

## BLACK THEOLOGY

How does Robert define what it means to be black when he speaks of a black theology? Why does he choose the term black and not Negro, Afro-American, or African-American? Roberts acknowledges this question is a question not only for whites in terms of their identifying people of African descent but also as an issue of self-identification for many black people. Roberts suggests that the term black has been a term loaded with shame in the past because of its meaning given by white authorities. Nonetheless, Roberts feels that the terms can also carry the message of a new consciousness for people in black skin. "For the present," he observes, "black says a great deal that needs saying." The term black makes it clear that black Americans "are not considered, nor are we treated, as

201 Roberts, *A Black Political Theology*, 217.
202 Ibid., 3.

most hyphenated Americans." Although America is a country "that promises freedom, equality, and justice for all," black Americans "are a huge minority that has not melted" into the "melting pot" that now constitutes the United States. Thus, in his view, "there is something profoundly meaningful in taking a term filled with shame and placing upon it a halo of glory." Indeed, he argues, it is of "great ethical and theological import" to take on the name "black Americans." He even contends that there is something "Christ-like" in "taking something shameful in the eyes of the white oppressor and investing it with pride and dignity." In the same way that "the cross, despised by Jews and Romans alike as a symbol of utter rejection, is for Christians a glorious symbol of God's matchless love" so the term black as defined by black theology "is a meaningful symbol of our new self-understanding as persons in black skin who are equal in nature and grace with all humans."[203] Those of us who are black, he contends, should be "black and proud."

## RECONCILIATION

Although Roberts identifies his work as a liberation theology, Roberts also insists that reconciliation between black and white Christians is not only possible but a divine requirement. "Christians," he contends, "are called to be agents of reconciliation."[204] Although he "shares much of the despair of the current impasse in black-white relations," he also strives to make the point that "human kind is wrapped up in a single garment of destiny." Thus, for him, not only "liberation" but also "reconciliation" must be the "goal" for all Christians.[205]

203 Roberts, *A Black Political Theology*, 190.
204 J. Deotis Roberts, *Liberation and Reconciliation*, rev. ed. (New York: Orbis Books, 1994), 34.
205 Ibid., 52.

Of particular import for Roberts is the work of Benjamin E. Mays, in particular his *The Negro's God as Reflected in His Literature*, a book written before "the more recent trends in black awareness, pride, and power" (of the sixties and seventies). What Roberts seeks to gain from Mays' work is his stress on the fact that God's revelation is a revelation for all people, and that it addresses the "whole" person, not merely an aspect of a person's life. In 1938, Mays, a president emeritus of Morehouse College, was interested not only in liberation but also in reconciliation; he was interested in how blacks and whites could find a "way to coexistence."[206] In this, he was concerned with what discrimination does to the one who practices it. He was concerned with the fact that the "hate destroys the hater as much as it does the hated."[207] Thus, as Mays sought to recover the humanity of blacks, he did not wish to make "second-class citizens out of whites."[208] He argues that if whites could recognize the dignity of blacks, they would also be surprised by their own humanity. Nonetheless, many blacks, including many devout lay Christians, ministers, even theologians, have given up these points. So many blacks have lost such faith in whites that they think that "to do anything decent toward the recovery of true humanity for blacks" means that they must seek "liberation" for blacks "by any means necessary."[209]

Nonetheless, Roberts argues that blacks must seek to go beyond merely their own "liberation" but that they must also work towards "reconciliation" and "peaceful coexistence" with whites. Of course seeking such reconciliation does not simply mean acquiescing to the controlled kind of integration many white churches confuse with reconciliation. Such a controlled integration simply seeks to have different races and ethnic groups occupy the same space without structural change taking place in the community, with white culture

206 Ibid., 51.
207 Ibid., 52.
208 Ibid.
209 Ibid.

remaining dominant. In order to move beyond controlled integration, churches also need to enable the poor and powerless to begin to experience empowerment. The dominant ethnic group needs to begin to eliminate oppressive practices and excluded ethnic groups need to be included in the community.

In order to achieve real reconciliation between blacks and whites, whites must come to the place where they both individually and collectively recognize their sin. Recognizing their sin does not require sending all white people through a guilt trip. It does mean that people need to come to terms with the facts and history of racism. They need to recognize the legacy of racism and the residues of this history as it still effects the present. The first step in recognizing this sin is naming it. They must recognize that "the life of the racist is a sinful, self-centered life." Racism is destructive of the human personality. The Christian life is one in which the "pride of racism" must be "overcome by faith." The characteristics of racism are "hatred, fear, anxiety, hostility, and self-glory."[210] The list of the racist is a "sinful, self-centered life." Racism is the purest form of self-glory because it exalts human beings over other human beings. Racism is the exaltation of the "finite" to the status of "infinite." Whites desire to be "as gods" to blacks.[211]

"Christian self-affirmation" is the solution to racism. It differs from all humanistic forms of self-realization, which promise self-fulfillment through striving. Rather, from a Christian standpoint, self-affirmation is about dedicating our lives to God; it is not striving. A true self-negation means that we are "crucified with Christ." The selfish ego dies. This sinful self must be "shattered" and "destroyed" before it can be renewed. The "I" turns away from itself to the "Thou." Once Christian racists recognize their sin of racism, they

210 Ibid.
211 Ibid., 56-57.

can open themselves up to "radical conversion." Their hatred of blacks can now become a "real love for them."[212]

Whites must honestly seek to make amends, at great personal sacrifice, to make amends for wrongs done to their black brothers and sisters.[213] And in seeking to make amends, whites must recognize both their personal complicity with racism and their "collective guilt." Of course, Roberts also observes that although "whites are guilty in this collective sense" and thus must repent of "their collective sin and accompanying guilt of oppression of black people, not all are guilty in a personal sense."[214] The question arises, however: Is each individual white person guilty of the social sins committed by a society dominated by white people? Roberts gives an affirmative answer. "When we say that all 'whites are racists,' do we mean guilty in a personal or collective sense? Racism is so deep-seated, however, on the unconscious level that such a categorical statement concerning guilt may be true to some extent."[215] In this, Roberts suggests racism as sin also involves an "unconscious or preconscious state." In this form, it is the most "insidious" and "destructive to the self and other selves." It is most deadly because on a conscious level, "the white racist is unaware of his or her true condition."[216] If God considers individuals and communities of people culpable for sins committed unintentionally or unknowingly, then Christian community must understand sin the same way. Roberts' contention is that these categories of sin are even more dangerous, "Preconscious racism is a type of (unpardonable) sin, for if one cannot recognize one's sin, if one has no sense of guilt or shame, one does not seek forgiveness through repentance."[217] If there is no repentance or forgiveness then reconciliation is unavailable.

212 Ibid., 52-53.
213 Ibid., 60.
214 Ibid., 57.
215 Ibid., 59.
216 Ibid., 58-59.
217 Ibid., 59.

Roberts has a nuanced analysis of white guilt for the sin of racism. Such guilt can be distinguished as being both personal and corporate; moreover, it can be distinguished as being both conscious and preconscious. When whites repent of their sin of racism, they need to repent not only for their sin of racism on a personal level, they must also repent of their corporate guilt of racism. Moreover, they must repent not only of the sins of racism that they are conscious of; they must also take responsibility for the sin of racism of which they are unaware. Repentance of the sin of racism must take both personal and corporate forms; it must be a repentance both of the racism one is conscious of and of the racism of which one is unaware.

But Roberts does not only deal with the need of whites to repent of their sins. He also argues that in order to overcome the damage done by racism and establish reconciliation between whites and blacks, blacks must be willing to make the move toward forgiving both individual and collective sin of whites. Roberts says, "Anyone who takes the Christian message of forgiveness seriously must be open to the possibility that reconciliation between blacks and whites is a possibility."[218] In this, Roberts makes it clear that the path for this all-inclusive forgiveness of whites must be paved not only by white repentance of their sin of racism, but whites must also be willing to move toward recognizing the dignity and establishing the full liberty of blacks. In calling for forgiveness of whites, Roberts makes it clear that he is not calling for "cheap grace." This is why he argues that true repentance on the part of whites – and a true conversion of their behavior, a true repentance of their sin of racism resulting in a changed way of life – must be the prerequisite of true reconciliation.

In making his case for forgiveness and reconciliation among blacks and whites, Roberts makes explicit that all people have sinned and that all people are the recipients of the salvation that comes

218 Ibid.

from Jesus Christ alone. This is where his theology is unique among theologians of the black theology movement. He stresses in a way that others do not the "universal" character of the gospel message – that the universal character of the gospel message about sin and grace applies for all people. He also stresses both the personal and corporate nature of sin and salvation – that salvation involves both conversion from sin on a personal level and our conversion of sin on a corporate level. It is because of Christ's offer of forgiveness for all people that blacks are able to forgive whites as sinners, who like them are also sinners saved by grace alone. This does not mean, in any way, as I have discussed above, a diminution of the sin of racism, whether on a personal or corporate level. It does, however, mean that there is the possibility for true repentance on the part of whites and the possibility of forgiveness on the part of blacks. The gospel heals the brokenness of sin both "within and without." For blacks, this healing will entail receiving the power to overcome the debilitating effects of racism and regaining a sense of autonomy and personal empowerment. For whites, this healing will entail repentance of their sin of racism and a transformation of their behavior so that they can treat blacks as equals. In making this argument, Roberts finally roots the "context of the questions for Christians insofar as racism is concerned" with one's "the inner life," which he describes as "the proper relation between oneself and the Lord of Life, even Jesus Christ." It is from "inner transformation – this 'saving' relationship" that "we may put all else in perspective." According to Roberts, "it is self-defeating to try to put the world together before we get ourselves together."[219] In sum, for Roberts, "there is a point where our Christian faith can lead us beyond the most robust humanism." Why? Because "we are heirs of a grace that enables as well as sanctifies. To love those who love you is a human act, but to love the oppressor and

219 Roberts, *Liberation and Reconciliation*, 63-64.

reject the oppression can be an act made possible by the agency of divine power alone."[220]

It is precisely with regard to his call for forgiveness on the part of blacks that Roberts has drawn strong criticism from his esteemed contemporary James Cone. In Cone's words, "Unfortunately, my black colleague, J. Deotis Roberts, has distorted the Christian view of black-white reconciliation precisely at this point. He implies that black people ought to forget their slavery and oppression and be prepared to join hands, in Christian love, with white oppressors.[221] In Cone's view, Roberts appears to be "letting whites off the hook" by suggesting an easy forgiveness in the absences of requiring changed hearts. Cone recognizes Roberts' call for repentance and dignity for people of color, but he believes that Roberts goes too far to when "he insists that blacks must hold up at all times the possibility for black-white interracial fellowship and cooperation. " If, indeed, "liberation is the precondition of reconciliation," then why, Cone asks, "should enslaved blacks assure white oppressors that we are ready to be reconciled when the latter have no intention of losing the chains of oppression?"[222]

The tension between these two men is interesting. They are saying essentially the same thing about a required repentance, meaning an honest change of heart. However, they differ in their approach to a solution. Cone stresses that "I am black first – and everything else comes after that. This means that I read the Bible through the lens of a black tradition of struggle and not as the objective Word of God"[223] By contrast, Roberts grounds his argument for racial reconciliation on an understanding of the universal character of the gospel and its import for all people. It is from the standpoint of the gospel's

220 Ibid., 59-60.
221 Cone, *God of the Oppressed*, rev. ed. (New York: Orbis Books, 1997), 219.
222 Ibid., 219.
223 Ibid., xi.

universal import that he develops his argument for black liberation and the possibility of reconciliation between blacks and whites, although he takes very seriously the particular standpoints of blacks and whites. In the next chapter, we examine John Perkins' approach to racial reconciliation, an approach that is similar to Roberts' in that it also seeks to ground an approach toward racial reconciliation on a universal understanding of the gospel's import for all people.

# CHAPTER FIVE

*John M. Perkins: A Model of Racial Reconciliation and Multicultural Community Development*

Roberts' black theology serves as a bridge between John M. Perkins' work and the black theologies of Cone and Wilmore. Although Perkins has not attempted to develop a black theology per se, his writings do develop a proposal for racial reconciliation that seeks not only to call for racial justice, but also to call for racial reconciliation. Like Roberts, his theology roots that call not only in an understanding of the specific experiences black Americans have experienced because of their race, but also in a more universal understanding of humanity's dignity before God as creatures and as those who, as sinners, can receive the gospel's message of grace for all. Nonetheless, even more than Roberts, he makes the case for an approach to racial relations that even more explicitly seeks to move beyond racial distinctions, even as it seeks to address the problem of racism.

## BIOGRAPHY

John M. Perkins is an American civil rights activist who has worked extensively on reconciliation and community development centered around the Christian gospel message. Born June 16, 1930, he grew up on a plantation as a sharecropper in the 1940s.[224] His mother, Maggie, died when he was six months old and his father, Jap, left the family about the same time. This left John, his two brothers, and two sisters to be raised by his grandmother who had already raised nineteen children. Later, when John was about four years old, he did see his father for a short time only to be abandoned by him for the rest of his life. For most of John's early years, living in Mississippi, his family was both sharecropping and bootlegging to make a living.

John learned his first lesson in economics when he was paid fifteen cents for a day of laboring for a white man who needed help bailing hay. He had expected a dollar and a half or two dollars. John says:

> I took the 15 cents. A dime and a buffalo nickel. And I couldn't do a thing. But I went away from there asking myself some questions. What happened to me? How was this white man able to exploit me? I took a long look at what had just happened to me and really began thinking about economics. That man had the capital: the land and the hay. And he had the means of production: the wagon and the horses. All I had were my wants and needs – and my labor. So I was exploited. I told myself, 'Tupy," this system is a system of capital. Get capital, control it and know how to use it. And if you're going to make it in this society, you've got to somehow or other get your hands on the means of production. Once you get the means of production, you can do good or evil with it. And this man done evil with it. He exploited you."[225]

This early experience would later have an influence on his stress on economic self-empowerment.

---

224 See John Perkins' *Let Justice Roll Down* (1976; repr. Grand Rapids: Regal Books, 2006) for a biography of John Perkins' life.

225 Ibid., 48-49.

In 1947, he moved from Mississippi to southern California at the urging of his family, who worried that he might be in danger following the fatal shooting of his brother, Clyde, by a police officer. His relatives in Hebron realized that John had been so embittered by his brother's murder that they sent him to Jackson fearing that he might do something that could cause him to end up like Clyde. Shortly after his move to Jackson, his family put together fifty dollars and set him off to California. In California John learned to take advantage of new opportunities. First, he was able to make good money. At the time working in a railroad foundry for $100 a week was real good money. He also learned to organize people while still in his teens.

In 1951, John was drafted into the United States Army. While on leave from the service, on a three-week pass, he was married to Vera Mae days before he left for his first tour of duty on Okinawa. In 1953, after his discharge from the Army, he and Vera Mae moved back to California. During the next few years, John developed a spiritual thirst. He tried studying with the Jehovah's Witnesses. He read some of Father Divine's material. He took a look at the Science of the Mind:

> We had a class in our house and went to Kingdom Hall – the whole bit. But after awhile, other things just sort of faded it out. The Lord was back of it all...But Vera Mae and I were both still searching for – something deeper and greater in life. I did some studies in Christian Science and read a lot about Father Divine. – I was trying everything. I know one thing. If I hadn't become a Christian, I would have become a Black Muslim. Their strict devotion and discipline have always appealed to me. I even came involved in Science of the Mind. And with this, I began to associate religion

with success. Success and money and "making it" were my religion, but I was not happy. I had no peace inside.[226]

However, it was when Spencer, his oldest son, came home from the local Protestant Catholic Church and invited his father to church that John attended a Christian church. Spencer's friend Calvin had been inviting him to the local Church of Christ for a while. Since John was more comfortable in a black church than in the local Protestant Catholic Church he starting attending Bethlehem Church of Christ Holiness with Vera Mae and his two children in 1957. It was at Bethlehem that John first understood the gospel and learned that it was profitable and interesting to study the Bible.

In 1960, he moved with his wife, Vera Mae, and children from California and to Mendenhall, where he began a Christian community development ministry in the rural Mississippi community. There, he helped to establish, among other things, a daycare center, a youth program, a church, a cooperative farm, a thrift store, a housing repair ministry, a health center, and an adult education program. In 1972, the Perkinses moved to Jackson, where they founded Voice of Calvary Ministries – another Christian community development ministry. The organization started a church, health center, leadership development program, thrift store, low-income housing development, and training center. From this ministry, other development projects started in the neighboring Mississippi towns of Canton, New Hebron, and Edwards.

In 1982, the family moved to Pasadena, California. There, Perkins founded Harambee Christian Family Center in Northwest Pasadena, a neighborhood with one of the highest crime rates in California. The center now runs programs including after school tutoring, Good News Bible Clubs, a technology center, summer

226 Ibid., 67.

day camp, youth internship programs, and a college scholarship program. In 1989, Perkins formed the Christian Community Development Association (CCDA), drawing on a nationwide group of Christian leaders to work in America's poor communities at a grass-roots level. The association held its first annual conference in Chicago in 1989 and has grown from 37 founding members to 6,800 individuals and 600 churches, ministries, institutions, and businesses in more than 100 cities. In 1992, Perkins began publishing *Urban Family*, a magazine emphasizing responsibility, affirming dignity, building moral character, and encouraging reconciliation. It soon had a circulation of 35,000. Later the magazine's name was changed to *Reconcilers Fellowship*. Perkins' eldest son led the magazine to publication. When he died in January 1998, the magazine was discontinued. In the fall of 1995, Perkins founded the Harambee Preparatory School (HPS), an elementary school providing academic programs for poor children.

After the death of his son in 1998, Perkins returned to Mississippi, and established the Spencer Perkins Center, the youth arm of the John M. Perkins Foundation. It has developed youth programs such as After School Tutorial, Summer Arts Camp, Junior and College Internship Program, Good News Bible Club, Young Life, and Jubilee Youth Garden. The foundation also has a housing arm, Zechariah 8, which provides affordable housing for low-to moderate-income families with a focus on single mothers.

### *Child Evangelism Fellowship*

An important influence on Perkins was his early involvement with the Child Evangelism Fellowship. Shortly after his conversion, his wife Vera Mae was reacquainted with Christ through a neighborhood friend, Wilnora Price, and a local Child Evangelism Fellowship ministry: "Vera Mae had been saved through Child Evangelism as a young girl and had always loved their use of flannel-boards. But Child Evangelism was new to me."[227]

John and Vera Mae where encouraged to get involved in this ministry through Wilnora. By this time, Perkins had a huge hunger for Bible teaching: however, his thoughts to attend a Bible college came to an abrupt end as he realized that because of his third grade education he would not be invited to attend. Alternative Bible training became available to John Perkins in the form of intense formal discipleship and tutoring by a Child Evangelism Fellowship leader named Wayne Leitch:

Every Tuesday night I sat with my white teacher, Mr. Wayne Leitch. God was taking me step by step. First He showed me black people changed by the gospel. Now He was showing me that it had power even for whites.

> Mr. Leitch didn't hold me back with any rigid ideas of what he thought my abilities ought to be. When he saw what I could handle, he offered to work with me during afternoons as well. My job by this time was in El Monte, where he lived; so I would stop by his school at three-thirty every day after work to learn, think and talk man to man, Christian to Christian. We met together like this for the next two years.[228]
>
> It was through two years of weekly intensive training at the El Monte Child Evangelism Training Center that John got his formal introduction to Biblical theology, doctrine, and an expositional methodology for handling the Word of God.

John Perkins' theology has to be described as conservative evangelical in nature. His original discipleship was under an evangelical organization that is conservative, if not fundamentalist.

227 Ibid., 74.
228 Ibid., 75.

With the foundations of his theology grounded in the doctrines of Child Evangelism Fellowship, John's ideas about Scripture took on Fundamentalist basics in two very important ways. First, John began to embrace a very high view of the Scriptures. Secondly, his study and preaching were expositional. The positive influence of the dispensationalists on John was in his Bible teaching. Dispensational theologians laid heavy emphasis on the verbal inspiration of the Bible, so it was important to them to thoroughly study and teach the exact meaning of every line of Scripture.[229]

Evidence of John's position on the Scripture as the divinely inspired Word of God can be seen or heard in his devotional bible address at the 2005 Christian Community Development Conference. At the conference, he affirmed that "The Holy Spirit is the author of God's Word." He affirmed that he takes the Bible to be "the inspired Word of God." He affirmed that he believes that the Bible is "a text book for life and that we have enough here to live the kind of life that God has called us to live." From the Bible, he notes, "we are to grow in grace and the knowledge of our Lord and Savior Jesus Christ." Indeed, he acknowledged that "the idea of the Christian Community Development movement was born out of the idea of trying to apply the word of God to our whole life, to our social life, our educational life, and all parts of our life. And that is why we call this movement holistic Christian community development."[230]

Perkins learned much from the theological framework and methods of Child Evangelism Fellowship. Under their influence, he "always did expository preaching and he used dispensational sources as his guides." His Bible was a Scofield Reference Bible, which places each passage of Scripture within the dispensational framework. As Stephen Berk notes in *A Time to Heal,* Perkins' "verse-

229 Stephen Berk, *A Time to Heal* (Grand Rapids: Baker Books, 1997), 98.

230 John Perkins, Friday Morning Bible Study (audio recording on *UrbanMinistry.org* , CCDA, 2005), www.urbanministry.org/audio/by/artist/john_perkins.html (accessed, February 2007).

-by-verse commentaries were by Harry Ironside, M. R. DeHaan, G. Campbell Morgan, Merrill Unger, and Dwight Pentecost." These dispensationalists gave him "a deep appreciation for the biblical text that enriched his teaching and preaching." In fact, "people with an intellectual bent, who felt alienated from black church emotionalism, were drawn to John."[231]

The Perkinses have been committed to Child Evangelism Fellowship throughout their entire ministry. After their ministry expanded to Pasadena, California the flannel graphs and teaching of Child Evangelism Fellowship was their primary methodology for reaching the children. As described in the book, *A Time to Heal*

> In October 1982 John and Vera Mae began to set up shop at Howard and Navarro [Pasadena, California]....Vera Mae became "Grandma Perkins" to each of the scores of children who came to her classes. And she introduced the children to "Grandpa Perkins." She held the first Child Evangelism classes in temporary quarters they patched hastily together in the garage of their house. The songs, prayers, missionary stories, and brightly illustrated Bible lessons on the flannel graph formed the structure of the Good News Clubs as Child Evangelism Fellowship had designed it.[232]

In the winter of 1996 the Child Evangelism Fellowship training was still important and an integral part of the Perkins ministry. Betty Perkins, John's youngest daughter, took a break from her ministry to receive intensive training in the Child Evangelism Fellowship methods.[233]

Nonetheless, although the CEF was influential on John, and on members of his family, he did not fully adopt the dispensational

231 Berk, *A Time to Heal,* 98.
232 Ibid., 297-98.
233 Ibid., 390.

fundamentalism the CEF presupposed. As Berk observes in *A Time to Heal,* Perkins "pondered the relationship of God's Word to the condition of black Mississippians," and "quickly recognized the glaring omissions in dispensational Fundamentalism." Although he "believed fervently in evangelism and conversion as the means and ground of faith, his deep personal awareness of poverty and oppression led him back into the world." Thus, he "veered away from the dispensational separation of spiritual from worldly concerns."[234]

### *The Jailhouse Experience*

In addition to CEF, another important factor shaping his theology was what he calls his "jailhouse experience." During the 1960s, Perkins had been involved with the civil rights movement as an agitation form of struggling against the oppression and injustice. But after he underwent a beating that took place in the Brandon, Mississippi, jail that night, his perspective had gone through a profound change. He describes this beating in vivid detail in *With Justice for All:*

> It was Saturday, February 7, 1970, about 6:30 p.m. The sun was just going down. Two vans driven by Louise Fox and Doug Huemmer were returning students to Tougaloo College near Jackson from Mendenhall where they had joined us in a civil rights march. In Plain, Mississippi, a few miles after the van rolled over the line separating Simpson County from Rankins County, the highway patrol car that had trailed them from Mendenhall flashed on its blue lights and cut in between the two vans signaling for Doug to pull over.
>
> A few minutes later our phone was ringing. It was Louise. "The people in Doug's van have been taken to the Brandon jail." Reverend Curry Brown, Joe Paul Buckley and I set out

234 Ibid., 97.

for the Rankin County Jail in Brandon to set bail for Doug and his group.

During the 45-minute drive up highway 49 my mind churned. Why had the policeman let Louise go? To call me? Was it a trap? Was another ambush waiting for us on highway 49?

We got to the county courthouse and jail and a highway patrolman showed us where to park. We had met no ambush on the highway. We got out of the car and told the patrolman, "We'd like to see the sheriff."

"Okay," he said. "You stay here and I'll go tell him you're here." Moments later out of the building came not Edwards but a dozen highway patrolmen. They searched us, arrested us and even before they got us to the building started beating us. It was an ambush after all!

Inside the jailhouse the nightmare only got worse. At least five deputy sheriffs and seven to twelve highway patrolmen went to work on us. Sheriff Edwards joined in.

Here's how I described that scene later in the court trial: "When I got to the jail and saw the people in jail, of course I was horrified as to why we were arrested and when I got in the jail Sheriff Jonathan Edwards came over to me right away and said, 'This is the smart nigger, and this is a new ballgame. You're not in Simpson County now; you are in Brandon.' He began to beat me, and from that time on they continued beating me. I was just beat to the floor and just punched and really beaten."

Manorris Odom, one of the Tougaloo students there, testified that Sheriff Edwards beat me so hard that his "shirt tail came out." During the beatings I tried to cover my head with my arms, but they beat me anyway till I was lying on the floor. Even then they just kept on beating and stomping me, kicking me in the head, in the ribs, in the groin. I rolled up into a ball to protect myself as best I could. And the beatings just went on and on.

> It got worse as the night wore on. One officer brought a fork over to me and said, "Do you see this?" And he jammed it up my nose. Then he crammed it down my throat. Then they beat me to the ground again and stomped on me.
>
> Because I was unconscious a lot of the time I don't remember a whole lot about the others. I do know that Doug and some of the students were beaten, and that Curry probably suffered the most of any of us.
>
> And I remember their faces so twisted with hate. It was like looking at white-faced demons. For the first time I saw what hate had done to those people. These policemen were poor. They saw themselves as failures. The only way they knew how to find a sense of worth was by beating us. Their racism made them feel like "somebody."
>
> When I saw that, I just couldn't hate back. I could only pity them. I said to God that night, "God, if you will let me get out of this jail alive" – and I really didn't think I would, maybe I was trying to bargain with Him – "I really want to preach a gospel that will heal these people, too."[235]

It was at this point that John Perkins understood that there was something else going on besides the civil rights of black people and other people of color. It was something *spiritual.*

John Perkins relayed in a private conversation with me that while he was laying on the floor the Brandon jail cell it had all come together: "I can't put it into words, but it was clear that the gospel is the answer." But, beyond that, he had also come to believe in his heart that God had called him to preach the gospel to white people as well as people of color:

> That night in the Brandon jail I had for the first time seen now the white man was a victim of his own racism. For the

235 Perkins, *Let Justice Roll Down,* 106-108.

> first time I wanted to bring him a gospel that could set him free. But that was only a start. I still harbored in my heart a deep-seated bitterness against whites for all they had done to me and my family. It went back to that night when Clyde was shot. Back beyond that to my mother's death. As my case went through the Mississippi courts and the majority of judges proved to be just as racist as the policemen who had almost killed me, my bitterness grew. There was no justice for a black man![236]

However, Perkins overcame the bitterness and entered into knowledge of God's grace that few of us experience.

Perkins reflects further on this experience that had such a profound impact for his later understanding of his ministry. As he lay in the hospital bed after his jailhouse experience, says that "God was showing me something, telling me something" through that experience. On the one hand, "there were blacks who had accepted our message." These blacks "had embraced the gospel"; they now "knew dignity." They now "walked taller than before." On the other hand, "there were whites who believed in justice." They lived, shared themselves, and "joined our community." I was able to see "with horror how hate could destroy me – destroy me more devastatingly and suddenly than any destruction I could bring on those who had wronged them. I could fight back, as many of my brothers had done. And if I did, how would be different from the whites who hate?"[237]

"And where would hating get me," he asks. "Anyone can hate. This whole business of hating and hating back. It's what keeps the vicious circles of racism going." That night "the Spirit of God worked on me as I lay in that bed." The image that came to his mind was the "image of the cross – Christ on the cross." And this Jesus on the cross "knew what I had suffered. He understood. And he

236 Ibid., 108.
237 Perkins, *Let Justice Roll Down,* 194.

cared." Because he had experienced it all himself, this Jesus, this One who had was in reality from God, had lived what he preached. He was arrested and falsely accused. "Like me, he went through an unjust trial. He also faced a lynch mob and got beaten. But even more than that, He was nailed to wooden planks and killed. Killed like a common criminal." At the crucial moment, "it seemed to Jesus that even God himself deserted him. The suffering was so great. He cried out in agony. He was dying." But when he looked at the "mob that had lynched him, he didn't hate them. He loved them. He forgave them. And he prayed God to forgive them." Perkins goes on to describe how "the Spirit of God kept working on me and in me until I could say with Jesus, 'I forgive them, too!"

At that point, Perkins describes how he promised that he would "return good for evil, not evil for evil." And he describes how God gave him the love he would need to fulfill his command to love your enemy. "Because of Christ God himself met me and healed my mind and my heard."[238] He describes how the "Spirit of God" helped him to really believe that "only in the love of Christ is there any hope for me and for those I had once worked so hard for." God gave him the strength and motivation "to rise up out of my bed and return to Mendenhall and spread a little more love around." It was out of that experience that he came to understand that there's something "built into" human beings that makes them want to be superior to others. "If the black man had the advantage, he'd be just as bad." This is why, he explains, "I can't hate the white man."[239]

We could say that at that moment, Perkins depersonalized racism. He realized that the sin of making oneself superior to another was a sin that all people could potentially commit, and that Christ's love

238 Ibid., 181.
239 Ibid., 181-182.

provided the reconciliation that enabled one not only to be reconciled to God but to be reconciled to other human beings as well.

## A STRATEGY FOR COMMUNITY DEVELOPMENT

### *Between Two Camps*

A central theme in *Let Justice Roll Down* is Perkins' attempt to move between two camps – the camps of the civil rights movement, on the one hand, and the evangelical, on the other: "One of the greatest tragedies of the civil rights movement," he observes, "is that evangelicals surrendered their leadership in the movement by default to those with either a bankrupt theology or no theology at all." In doing this, the vast majority of "Bible believing Christians ignored a great and crucial opportunity in history for genuine ethical action." The evangelical church, to which Perkins belonged, "had not gone on to preach the *whole* gospel."[240]

So he decided to act, and this placed him squarely between two camps. Like evangelicals, he also presupposed that he needed to start "with the gospel that calls men to Christ for forgiveness and God's strength." The search for justice cannot merely a search based on coercion or, in his words, "human manipulation." Yet, at the same time, the church, relying solely on "so-called 'spiritual' manipulation alone," cannot effect justice.[241]

On the one hand, at the heart of Perkins' concern is that the black community faces problems related not merely to structures but also to values. The black community had experienced two hundred years of slavery, followed by generations of "economic exploitation, political oppression, racial discrimination and educational deprivation." This had created within black people "feelings of inferiority, instability, and

240 Ibid., 195.
241 Ibid., 99.

social dependency." Such "negative values" in a people deprives them of "any true sense of self-worth, or any real sense of self-identity." The result is "negative behavior" that is, in the end, "self-destructive in its effect." Dehumanizing values tend to produce destructive behavior. Perkins saw clearly that "integration, equal opportunity, welfare, charity and all other such programs" fail if they failed to deal with the negative values that left black communities "spiritually bankrupt." What was needed was something that could counter this spiritual bankruptcy. Thus, for Perkins, "the gospel of Jesus Christ, with its power to transform people by the renewing of their minds" (see Rom. 12:22) is of primary importance to the black community.[242]

At the same time, with regard to the white evangelical church, Perkins was also aware of their need to relate their professed faith to matters of social concern. He also felt a need to make white Christians aware of their responsibility for the racial problems all Americans face. The problem he had to face was not merely a black problem. White people had also failed "to allow the gospel to speak fully to them," to their lifestyles and behavior patterns that are often "exploitive and unjust." Indeed, Perkins notes, "if Christ is Savior, he must be Lord – Lord over such areas as spending, radical attitudes, and business dealing." The gospel must penetrate "the white consciousness as well as the black consciousness."[243]

In *Beyond Charity: The Call to Christian Community Development,* Perkins explicitly relates his own approach to the black theology movement of the sixties and seventies. In his view, "Black theology has not adequately answered the question of what liberation looks like."[244] Because it was "born in rebelling against European theology," it still presupposes the idea of a "divided

242 Ibid., 101.
243 Ibid., 102.
244 John M. Perkins, *Beyond Charity: The Call to Christian Community Development* (Grand Rapids: Baker Books, 1993). 41.

church." By contrast, Perkins wants to move towards defining the marks of an "authentic church," one that is rooted in the "living gospel." The gospel, Perkins argues, is "the visible demonstration of the love of God. It is the manifestation of God's love in the world," a love that is freely offered to us. Indeed, he goes on, "the death of Christ on the cross was the ultimate way that God showed his love for us." And now, as result of God's love, we have the "wonderful task of manifesting God's love to the world. We are the agents through whom God demonstrates this love today." From this understanding of the gospel, we can see that the love of God is about "incarnation" and "transformation." God's ultimate demonstration of his love was through the incarnation of Christ: "We have seen his glory, glory as of the only Son from the Father, full of grace and truth" (John 1:14). Jesus Christ came to us, lived among us, and died for us. By knowing Jesus, God in man, the disciples were able to know God: "Whoever who has seen me has seen the Father" (John 14:9). And now, today, God is incarnated within and among us. We now are the hands and feet of Christ in the world.[245]

### *Felt Needs*

This incarnational and transformational theology is embodied in the strategy for community development that Perkins outlines in several of his books.[246] As we have seen, for Perkins, "evangelism is not enough."[247] Ministry must always address the "felt needs" of the communities it seeks to serve. Since felt needs differ person to person and place to place, one can only minister effectively, Perkins observes, if one discovers and identifies what those needs are in each situation. Nonetheless, over the years, he has found three inherent

245 Ibid., 58.

246 See, e.g., Perkins, *With Justice for All: A Strategy for Community Development* (Grand Rapids: Regal Books, 2007).

247 Ibid.

needs to be universal. The extent to which a person has these needs met is the extent to which that person develops, grows, and secures a sense of dignity.[248]

The first need is "the need to belong." We all have a need to belong to someone and to something. "In the poorer areas of our nation," Perkins notes, "families are often torn apart, love is scarce, and people live with a sense of hopelessness and a bitterness toward life." Individuals in these communities not only want to belong, but they want to sense that the world around – on the streets and at home – is not hostile to them. In fact, Perkins goes so far as to say that "this need to belong is at the heart of the urban gang problem."[249]

The second need is "the need to be significant and important – to be somebody." This is especially for the task of developing indigenous leaders, a theme of Perkins' work. We must develop such leaders, Perkins observes, in a way that affirms their dignity as human beings. And in doing so, we must motivate people "to take responsibility for their lives." Perkins is highly critical of the welfare mentality, which, in his view, incapacitates people by making them dependent on others. "It is amazing to see how these children," he observes, "who hear and experience so much negative reinforcement, thrive when they begin to believe that they are special."[250]

The third need is the "need for a reasonable amount of security." Black communities are often found in places that are not secure places to live. If Christian community development is to be successful, then a major focus needs to be on making families feel secure in their own neighborhoods. Perkins comments: "One of the most gratifying things for me is to see the children, who used to live in terror, begin to play in the streets."[251]

---

248 Perkins, *Beyond Charity*, 35.
249 Ibid., 35.
250 Ibid., 36.
251 Ibid., 36.

### *The Three R's of Community Development*

In order to respond to a community's felt needs, Perkins has developed what he calls the "three R's of community development." These principles are described in *With Justice for All* and are at the heart of his strategy for Christian community development.[252] The genius of Perkins' ministry model is not in its theological articulation for a need to break down centuries of assumptions consistent with a racialized society, but in the practical manifestation of the theology in the ministry itself. His Christian Community Development Association, which is founded on the three R's model of Relocation, Reconciliation, and Redistribution, is creating options for people, options that are being played out in urban and suburban communities alike.

The first R is *relocation.* To minister effectively to the poor, he argues, we individual Christians and corporate church communities must relocate to communities of need. By living as a neighbor with the poor, the needs of the community become our own. Shared needs and friendships became a bridge not only for communicating the good news of Jesus Christ, but also for working together for better conditions in the community. This according to Perkins is what it means to part of the Body of Christ, being like Christ who "became flesh and dwelt among us" (see John 1:14).[253] Such relocation will mean different things to different people. For some, it means "going back" to one's hometown. For others, it will mean moving from the "outside in, to uplift the people who are there."[254]

The second R is *reconciliation.* The gospel has the power to reconcile people to God and to each other. Humanity's reconciliation to God through Jesus Christ is clearly the heart of the gospel. But we must be reconciled to each other. Reconciliation across racial,

252 For a discussion of the three "R's," see Perkins, *With Justice for All* and *Beyond Charity.*

253 Perkins, *With Justice for All,* 55.

254 Perkins, *Beyond Charity,* 36.

cultural, and economic barriers is not an optional aspect of the gospel. We need one another. God commands us to love and forgive one another. Our love for one another demonstrates to the world that we are indeed Jesus' disciples (see John 13:35). We must be reconciled to God and other human beings.[255] The love and forgiveness of the gospel compels us, Perkins argues, to be reconciled to God and to each other across racial, cultural, social, and economic barriers. At the heart of such reconciliation is the recognition that "love is stronger than hate" and that the goal of the gospel is always a "reconciled community."[256]

The third R is for *redistribution.* Christ calls us to share with those in need. This calls for redistributing more than our goods. It means sharing our skills, our time, our energy, and our gospel in ways that empower people to break out of the cycle of poverty and assume responsibility for their own needs. Perkins offers very practical suggestions for how such redistribution might take place. We must organize business enterprises within the community of need, he contends, that will be owned by a broad base of people. This will mean using such methods as cooperative, mutual saving and loan associations, and credit unions. The goal of such redistribution is not "absolute equality," but a more "equitable distribution of resources."[257] Many so-called poverty programs are ineffective because they fail to provide the actual resources to help people break out of cycles of poverty and actually take responsibility for their own lives.[258]

Perkins emphasizes the connection among the three R's: Relocation, Reconciliation, and Redistribution. In his introduction to *With Justice for All*, he makes this clear. The answer to redistribution must begin with relocation and reconciliation. There

---

255 Perkins, *With Justice for All*, 51, 55.
256 Perkins, *Beyond Charity*, 36.
257 Perkins, *With Justice for All*, 56.
258 Perkins, *Beyond Charity*, 46.

is no *redistribution* without *relocation* and *reconciliation.* "The most important thing we have to redistribute," he notes, "is ourselves." We cannot achieve justice by "long distance." Of course, not all are called to "go"; some are called to "send." But his basic strategy begins with the "redistribution of skilled people." Only after people are "redistributed," he argues, "can we employ money in ways that produce development rather than dependency." In his view, redistribution is not primarily about "giving poor people money." Rather, it is primarily about "reconciliation and becoming one with the people in ministry."[259]

Nowhere in John Perkins' work will one find a direct statement about the mandate for the deconstruction of racialization. However, the assumption is found throughout his work. Each of the three cornerstone principles for the Christian Community Development Association – Relocation, Reconciliation, and Redistribution – assume the deconstruction of racial, ethnic, and cultural typology. When asked if the rich must relocate by leaving their comfortable surrounding and actually move physically into a poor neighborhood Perkins says, "Yes, our best attempts to reach people from the outside will patronize them. Our best attempts will psychologically and socially damage them. We must live among them. We must become one with them. Their needs must become our needs."[260] We must live among them rather than avoid them because of the perceived genetic or cultural inferiority ideas driven by racialization. Racialization suggests differences where the relocation doctrine suggests equality. When a suburban Christian chooses a ministry among those who are aching without becoming one with them,[261] patronization takes place even when the do-gooder is performing the same ministry function as the relocater. When ministry is performed out of obligation and

259 Perkins, *With Justice for All*, 179.
260 Perkins, *With Justice for All*, 90.
261 Ibid., 90.

not out of true love, if we do "law justice" instead of "love justice" the fruit will be different. Ministry performed out of love produces a sense of acquired responsibility for suffering people and an experience of being accountable to the people being reached.

Attempts at the racial integration of a community without first deconstructing the racialized worldview have not empowered people of color. It in fact divided the communities of color, weakening them. The weakening is a result of leaving the most vulnerable members in concentrated areas while those with economic and educational means move to the more desirable suburbs. Perkins comments that during the 1960s many black Americans who were upwardly mobile thrived. They obtained education and skills, which gave many good jobs for the first time. Ironically, he observes, the very elimination of the injustices that had kept upwardly mobiles back "helped to create the situation we have in the inner cities today." Because of the Fair Housing Act of 1968, many upwardly mobile blacks moved out of the inner cities. Now a part of the middle class, they bought houses outside of black neighborhoods, returning only "to administer programs for the people still living there." Not only did this make it difficult for those who had moved out to identify with the pain of the urban poor, but their very jobs, Perkins notes, "depended on the poor, making them 'poverty brokers' of sorts."[262]

The civil rights movement may have made segregation illegal. But it did not address fundamental issues facing the black community. The riots of the late 1960s functioning as the culmination of the civil rights movement were only a precursor for the riots of the 1990s signaling the fact that the changes in the 1950s and 1960s were not deep enough. The nation remained racialized. The long-term effects of this process have been the devastation of inner city communities with particular destruction being done in communities of color. It is

262 Perkins, *Beyond Charity,* 9-10.

precisely the need for a much deeper transformation that Perkins' program of community development seeks to address.

### *Urban-Suburban Partnerships*

In his recent work, John Perkins has sought to work on suburban and urban partnerships. In *Linking Arms, Linking Lives: How Urban-Suburban Partnerships Can Transform Communities*, a book co-authored with others working on community development, Perkins broadens the scope of program for community transformation based on the three R's. Drawing on a growing network of development practitioners, pastors, and theologians, this book focuses on the experiences of partnership between urban and suburban groups in order to provide both theological foundations and practical guidelines for those interested in partnering effectively.

Perkins argues that if partnerships are to have a chance, both partners "must mutually submit to Christ's lordship and commit to God's justice." It is precisely this mutual grounding that is the basis for making the partnership a truly equal exchange. Indeed, Perkins asserts, a true partnership must be an equal exchange: "Suffice it to say here that both sides must strive for equality, mutual respect, and mutual power – the stuff of true partnership – and they must resist the very real inequality that exists in the world."[263]

Such partnership is the ground for any kind of true reconciliation among people of different backgrounds. Perkins acknowledges that reconciliation is a "rich theological and sociopolitical concept."[264] But he also maintains that reconciliation is not simply a theory. Rather, it "compels us to view one another with dignity, equality, and mutual

263 John M. Perkins et al., *Linking Arms, Linking Lives: How Urban-Suburban Partnerships Can Transform Communities* (Grand Rapids: Baker Books, 2008), 80.
264 Perkins et al., *Linking Arms*, 66.

respect." It compels us to overcome the sentiments that have given to our being what Emerson and Smith have called a "racialized society"—"from the injustice endured by Native Americans to black slavery and Jim Crow laws to Japanese relocation."[265] A racialized society is one in which "intermarriage rates are low, residential separation and socioeconomic inequality are the norm, our definitions of personal identity and our choices of intimate associations reveal racial distinctiveness, and where "we are never unaware of the race of a person with whom we interact." In short, a racialized society is a society wherein race matters profoundly for differences in life experiences, opportunities, and social relationships.[266] By contrast, communities that are grounded in true partnership will seek to overcome the characteristics of a racialized society. They will seek the equal exchange of true partnerships. They strive for "equality, mutual respect, and mutual power"[267] even as they address people's "need to be one with each other."[268]

We can glean six principles from Perkins' proposal for building meaningful partnership between urban and suburban communities. First, in order to build urban-suburban partnerships it is imperative to come to a full acceptance of human equality before God. Although differences exist among people – based on various differences (race, class, gender, and the like) – these differences do not take away from their fundamental humanity before God and before one another. Second, the members in a multicultural community intentionally blending urban and suburban culture, must begin, and continue, to undergo a process of disconnecting from the previously held assumptions that have led to their being racialized, that is, to their categorizing one another on the basis of racial differences. Third,

265 Ibid., 66. See the quotation in Michael O. Emerson and Christian Smith, *Divided by Faith: Evangelical Religion and the Problem of Race in America* (New York: Oxford University Press, 2001).
266 Ibid., 66-67.
267 Perkins, *Linking Arms*, 80-81.
268 Perkins, *With Justice for All*, 59.

in doing this, it is important not only to deconstruct racialization but also to dismantle racism. This dismantling process requires becoming aware of the assumptions we bring when we meet those of different racial and ethnic groups. In other words, what has it meant to be white? What has it meant to be black? What has it meant to be yellow, brown, or red? The urban-suburban community partnership requires an understanding of these assessed values and intentionality build policy and develop new traditions that counter these old assessed values. Fourth, players in the multicultural urban-suburban partnership must address the victimization and pain experienced by all parties involved. This victimization has been caused not only by the biased and racist practices in the past by also by the failed attempts to address these sins. This should include the experiences of whites (as they undergo recognition of their own complicity in racism) as well as blacks (as they begin to experience a deeper sense of their own empowerment). Fifth, a multicultural community must struggle to assign new meanings and develop new policies governing relationships consistent with our identity in Christ. This does not eliminate legitimate cultural, gender, and ethnic distinctions; nonetheless, it recognizes those distinctions in light of our deeper unity and equality within the body of Christ. Finally, members in the urban-suburban multicultural community must make a commitment to the will of God and to conduct their lives with their brothers and sisters in Christ in ways that are consistent with the truth of God revealed will in his Word.[269]

## THE GOSPEL AND ITS IMPLICATIONS FOR JUSTICE

At the heart of Perkins' work is the assumption that we were created in God's image for fellowship with God and with one another. He states this succinctly in *Restoring at Risk Communities:*

269 These principles are gleaned from themes discussed in Perkins, *Living Arms, Living Lives.*

> Being created in God's image has many implications, one of which is the close relationship that God has with human beings. . . . Mankind was created to have fellowship with God and cannot be truly human otherwise. Yet sin has destroyed our relationship with God . . . God showed the full extent of his love for us by sending Jesus Christ to restore the relationship that was destroyed in the Garden.[270]

The focus in this statement is the relationship that Adam had with God in the garden. It was a relationship lost due to sin. When Adam lost this precious relationship, his identity changed. He was no longer the son of God; he was now the son of the Devil. So, what is the gospel? Christ died for our sins. The gospel is a historic event. It is an event that took place in time and space where Jesus Christ was crucified. What happened at the fall? Adam acquired guilt because of his disobedience but he also lost his identity because of disobedience.

The gospel is the key to deconstructing racialization, dismantling racism and effecting reconciliation in the body of Christ for the glory of God. A gospel sufficient to effect healing in all of these areas must be a gospel that speaks directly, not only to our broken relationship to God, but speaks to our broken relationships on a horizontal plane as well. We have seen how the overwhelming majority of conservative evangelical Christians place the emphasis of the gospel message on our broken relationship with God and, at best, view the issues on the horizontal plane as a by-product of salvation and secondary to the gospel message. We have also seen how the seminal proponents of Black Theology place the emphasis of biblical teaching on the lack of social and political justice in the experience of black and other people of color. They insist that white people need to repent and come to terms with their racist agendas. While these emphases have their

---

270 John M. Perkins, *Restoring At Risk Communities: Doing It Together and Doing It Right* (Grand Rapids: Baker, 1995) 28.

place, they both miss the richness of the gospel message sufficient for reconciliation on both the vertical and the horizontal planes.

John Perkins has responded to the objections of conservative evangelicals, whose teaching is consistent with those of men like Billy Graham, suggesting that social issues were important, but only as the fruit or secondarily to evangelism and the gospel message, by offering the definition of the gospel as, "the visible demonstration of God's love."[271] Perkins insists that the gospel includes a social dimension. The gospel manifests God's love in the world. "This love is freely offered to us. The death of Christ on the cross was the ultimate way that God showed his love for us. Now we who believe in God have the wonderful task of manifesting God's love to the world. We are the agents through whom God demonstrates this love today."[272]

John Perkins has been frequently criticized for this understanding of the gospel by conservative evangelicals. In *Beyond Charity*, he describes one such challenge. While presenting a workshop in Houston, he gave his definition of the gospel as "the demonstration of God's love." At that workshop, a pastor in the back of the room raised his hand and said, "I disagree with your definition of the gospel." He then quoted 1 Corinthians 15:1-5 where Paul says, "I want to remind you of the gospel I preached to you. . . . By this gospel you are saved, if you hold firmly to the word I preached to you . . . that Christ died for our sins according to the Scriptures, that he was buried, that he was raised on the third day according to the Scriptures, and that he appeared to Peter, and then to the Twelve" (NIV). This man insisted that Perkins' definition of the gospel required more of a believer than the Bible itself did, since the Bible to him said that all a person had to do in order to be saved was "hold firmly" to the gospel

271 Perkins, *Beyond Charity,* 58.
272 Ibid., 58.

as it is presented in 1 Corinthians 15.[273] Then another person spoke up. He said that his grandmother was "the sweetest woman in the whole world, that he was sure she was saved and going to heaven, but that she had a tiny problem: She was racist against black people." "How can the love of God abide in you if you hate your brother?" I asked, alluding to 1 John 4:20. She is still going to heaven, they insisted, even if she never stops hating black people, because she has believed the gospel.[274] This theology of the gospel that allows people to hate their neighbor while claiming to believe in the gospel[275] is an impotent theology that will do nothing to deconstruct racialization, dismantle racism, or effect reconciliation on horizontal plane. If we take 1 John 3:15 seriously, that "Everyone who hates his brother is a murderer, and you know that no murderer has eternal life abiding in him," it is questionable as to whether this grandmother's theology of the gospel has the power to reconcile the sinner to God.

There has often been a divide in the church between those who are concerned with personal salvation and those who are concerned with social justice. In his presentation at the 1998 Christian Community Development Association conference, Perkins seeks to recover faith and works together. He seeks to bridge the divide in the church between those who did social work, whom we call liberal, and those who talk about God, whom we call fundamentalist or evangelical. "But now," he observes, "what we are trying to do is bring faith and works back together. We are trying to bring the evidence of our faith by our good works. And so we are here to do God's work."[276] At a 2006 Christian Community Development Association's national conference, Perkins made a similar claim when he asserted that justice is of paramount concern to God: "Justice," he asserted, "is the all-inclusive concern

273 Ibid., 68.
274 Ibid., 68.
275 Ibid.
276 John M. Perkins, Friday Morning Bible Study (audio recording on YouTube, CCDA, 1998) www.youtube.com/watch?v=QVDf9TUK9xM (accessed, February 2007).

that God has. To think about being Christian and not thinking about or understanding justice is to not be a Christian. Because we were left here on earth to be God's justice agents on earth both in the way we live and the way we reflect it on society. Justice was the motivation for God's redemption.[277]

Like many people of color in the battle for freedom, equality, and justice in the United States, John Perkins founds some of his challenge on the Declaration of Independence. His argument, like many who argue the point, is that the "created equal" clause should have guaranteed justice for all men living in the community to be called the United States of America. Perkins argues that that which was stated to be inalienable was never applied to all of the members of the community:

> "We hold these truths to be self-evident, that all men are created equal . . ." With these words the Declaration of Independence of the United States of America holds out the noble promise of justice for all. Yet the very signing of this landmark of human freedom betrayed its own promise. For among its signers stood men who at that very moment owned other men. Justice for all didn't really mean justice for all; it meant justice for some. The "inalienable" right of liberty belonged only to the privileged.[278]

Perkins argues that the current socio-economic gap and education gap existing among people of color and whites is evidence of the lack of justice being played out in America. His concern is not that people do not have the same positions but that they do not have the same options or equal opportunity: "To this day our nation has not lived up to its goal of justice for all. Would anyone claim that a child trapped in the ghetto has equal access to quality education as

277 John M. Perkins, Saturday Morning Bible Study (audio recording on *UrbanMinistry.org*, CCDA, 2006) www.urbanministry.org/audio/by/artist/john_perkins.html (accessed February 2007).
278 Perkins, *With Justice for All,* 11.

his suburban counterpart? Would anyone claim that the teenage girl in the ghetto has the same chance of getting a summer job as the girl from an affluent family? Or that the ethnic young adult, deprived of good education and job experience, has an equal chance of making it in the American job market?" For Perkins, poverty is much more than simply the lack of money; it is the lack of options: "For millions in our land there is not justice. For them, 'equal opportunity' is at best an elusive dream; at worst a cruel taunt."[279]

In addition to addressing the problem of injustice, we can see that Perkins has also moved towards a stance that explicitly rejects the very foundation of racialization. Quoted in a *Christianity Today* article, Perkins says, "There is no biblical basis for a black, white, Hispanic, or Asian church."[280] Two important ideas drive John Perkins' successful work with white, conservative evangelicals. First, he is a conservative evangelical himself with a conservative theology, without which most conservative evangelicals will not even offer a hearing. The second idea sets him apart as a black conservative Christian practitioner: Perkins is one of the few in conservative circles to operate from a model that first, does not acquiesce to the shortsighted white churchmen who want reconciliation without addressing the issues of justice historically or the legacy and residue of injustice present systemically in our ecclesiastical institutions. At the same time, Perkins has managed to emphasize the gospel in such a way as to disarm most white guilt. He accomplishes this balancing act by coming very close to deconstructing racialization. Although Perkins does not develop a fully articulated theology in support of deconstructing the social construct, he treats white Christians from the point of view that "whiteness" as a socially constructed idea and people from European descent are not one and the same within the construct. "Whiteness" is guilty of the evil atrocities of

279 Ibid., 11-12.
280 Andres Tapia, "The Myth of Racial Progress," *ChrTo*, 4 October 1993, 18.

racism. However, each individual from European descent is given the opportunity to prove their heart's affections.

# CHAPTER SIX

## *Towards Deconstructing Racialization and Dismantling Racism in the Evangelical Church*

### A SUMMARY OF THE ARGUMENT

The purpose and focus of this study has been to examine John Perkins' model of racial reconciliation in light of some of the major players in black American history, including Booker T. Washington, W.E.B. DuBois, James Cone, Gayraud Wilmore, and J. Deotis Roberts. All of the men mentioned had similar basic outcomes in mind. Each wanted to end racism. Each wanted political, economic, and social justice for all people and, in particular, people of color. However, each of them came to the table with slight differences in their basic worldview, giving rise to slightly different desired outcomes and slightly different strategies employed to produce the desired outcomes.

Born into slavery, Washington's major goal was to better the economic conditions of black people. Although his work for economic stability for blacks was important, his decision to compromise became paradigmatic for his generation and the generation of black people that followed. DuBois challenged Washington's position of compromise and took the stance of an agitator, seeking legal equality for blacks. Although he rejected a biological argument for the maintenance of racial groups, he nonetheless maintained that it was important for blacks to avoid assimilation in order to preserve a sense of their own identity as members of a race.

The black theology movement of the twentieth century sought to criticize white theology, bringing to the fore what they saw as its racist implications, and articulate a theology that was relevant to black experience. Cone emphasized the ways in which black theology could undergird a healthy understanding of black power. Wilmore emphasized the need to articulate an Africentric theology that could adequately address the needs of black Americans. But in defining black theology over against white theology, these thinkers, in spite of their profound critique of racism, were still defining their theological task in profoundly racialized terms. Roberts moves in a slightly different direction with his emphasis on the universal import of the gospel and his attempt to define a black theology of liberation and reconciliation in terms of that universal import.

The distinctiveness of Perkins' work lies in the fact that he seeks not only to grapple with grapple with racism, but also to move toward a stance that seeks to disempower racialization by what we could call "depersonalizing" racism. This depersonalization of racism takes place when Perkins makes the distinction between the social, political, and ethical construct of whiteness and blackness and what people really are. This disconnect allows racism to be objectified and attacked by all members of the Christian community. With the social, political, and ethical constructs placed in position rather than real people, guilt for racism can be understood objectively and assessed in terms of the interplay between real people and the constructs. Culpability then, for individuals, can be assessed to those who have earned guilt. The work of building community has the potential of going forward without the racially and culturally diverse membership attacking each other. Perkins' model allows for the development of a truly reconciled, multiracial, multi-ethnic, and multicultural Christian community. The model establishes the church in terms of their identity in Christ, based on the reconciliation with God and with one another accomplished on the cross. The only way to effectively destroy racism is through the dismantling of racialization. This is the strength of John M. Perkins' work, which presents an alternative to the other black leaders because his model effectively addresses the problem of racialization. His work not only addresses the problem of racism; it also addresses the problem of racialization.

Perkins' approach addresses Washington's concerns for economic reforms. He addresses DuBois' concerns for legal equality and for Negro identity, even as he argues as well for the possibility of a reconciled multicultural community that works together without obliterating cultural distinctions. His approach grapples with the concerns of Cone, Wilmore, and Roberts that simply de-racializing European based theological constructs will not guarantee the theology's ability to address the experiences of people who have been marginalized historically. Perkins' model does not acquiesce to the weaknesses and shortcoming of European theologians, but rather faces the weaknesses in Eurocentric theological expressions by offering a more accurate understanding of the gospel by not overlooking the implications of the fall and the meaning of Christ's death for all. Perkins asks the appropriate questions of the text that need to be asked to address the experiences of people of color and the poor.

Nonetheless, he seeks to develop a ministry praxis that speaks to and challenges the needs of people of color and the poor, on the one hand, and the White, Western, and Wealthy who are comfortable in their socio-economic status, on the other. Thus, he seeks to not only address racism, but also the racialization that is its by-product. He challenges racialization, the worldview that attempts to use biology to organize humans into “so called” racial groups. In particular, he challenges the way this worldview still dominates much of the conservative evangelical church’s theology and practice, which fails to see the import of the gospel for issues of injustice and racism. He seeks to relate our vertical reconciliation with God to our horizontal reconciliation with one another. He seeks to demonstrate that the radically new identity we have in Christ, because of what Christ has done for us, has profound implications for how we treat one another in very concrete social, political, and economic terms. In sum, Perkins has offered a model that brings both vertical and horizontal reconciliation together in the gospel with the potential of breaking racialization’s strangle hold in the church. With a model that emphasizes identity “in Christ” and depersonalizes racism by demonstrating a distinction between the social and political constructs of whiteness and blackness and real people, Perkins provides realistic tools for deconstructing racialization, dismantling racism, and providing reconciliation among ethnic groups in the evangelical church.

## IMPLICATIONS FOR JUSTICE AND RECONCILIATION

In the following section, I would like to draw out some of the theological implications implicit in Perkins’ work. I organize my comments around two main emphases in his work, emphases that inform his approach to racial integration: justice and reconciliation.

### *Justice*

Justice is a central theme in Perkins’ work, as indicated by the titles of some of his books: *Let Justice Roll Down*, *With Justice for*

*All.*[281] His understanding of justice broadens the concept of human sin beyond a strictly individual understanding of sin. This broadening of the concept of sin is actually deeply rooted in biblical themes.

Evangelicals typically limit their understanding of Adam's sin as acquired of individual guilt. Therefore, when Paul talks about the imputation of Adam's sin in Romans 5, he is talking about Adam's guilt being imputed to the individual person with no explicit corporate implications or responsibility. In much conservative evangelical thinking, the gospel is limited to a propositional truth statement that must be believed. This thinking has had a significant effect on the praxis of the church with particular implications since the turn of the twentieth century. Conservative evangelicals find themselves in a conundrum. How do we address the question of social justice? How do we think about action on a horizontal plane – man to man? Should the gospel be limited to the proposition that sin is only personal and individual, that one should love the Lord God with all of our hearts, souls, and minds, and that reconciliation takes place only on the vertical plane? What about loving our neighbors as ourselves? What about the teaching in the Sermon on the Mount?

This struggle to locate the idea of justice as a part of the church's mission has been a historic one. Part of the struggle has been in defining the word translated "justice" or "righteousness." Bosch wrestled with the translation of *dikaiosyne* in an attempt to provide a working definition.

> The translation of *dikaiosyne* poses problems, however, at least in English. It can refer to justification (God's merciful act of declaring us just, thus changing our status and pronouncing us acceptable to him), or to righteousness (a preeminently religious or spiritual concept: an attribute of

281 See John M. Perkins, *Let Justice Roll Down* (Grand Rapids: Regal Books, 2006) and *With Justice for All: A Strategy for Community Development* (Grand Rapids: Regal Books, 2007).

> God or a spiritual quality that we receive from God), or to justice (people's right conduct in relation to their fellow human beings, seeking for them that to which they have a right). Most English New Testament translations reveal a bias toward the second meaning. Often the word "justice" does not appear at all in an English New Testament – with important consequences. One discovers this if one translates *dikaiosyne* in the sayings of Jesus alternatively with "righteousness" and "justice". The fourth beatitude (Mt 5:6) may then refer either to those who hunger and thirst after (spiritual) righteousness and holiness, or to those who long to see that justice be done to the oppressed. By the same token, the "persecuted" of Matthew 5:10 may be suffering because of their religious devoutness (righteousness), or because they champion the cause of the marginalized.[282]

Here, the connection can be seen between the Greek propositional idea of the gospel and a broader understanding of the gospel. The first two translation options, justification (God's merciful act of declaring us just, thus changing our status and pronouncing us acceptable to him), and righteousness (a preeminently religious or spiritual concept: an attribute of God or a spiritual quality that we receive from God), suggest ideas consistent with limiting the gospel to vertical reconciliation between man and God. Both options limit the effect of the gospel to changing our status before God. The third option, justice (people's right conduct in relation to their fellow human beings, seeking for them that to which they have a right), broadens reconciliation to a horizontal relationship between and among human beings. Bosch settled on the idea of using both righteousness and justice to translate *dikaiosyne* into English: "Perhaps, however, we should not allow ourselves to choose between 'righteousness' and 'justice' when seeking for the meaning of *dikaiosyne.* Our problem may, rather, lie in the fact that the English language is unable

282 David J. Bosch, *Transforming Mission: Paradigm Shift in Theology of Mission* (New York: Orbis Books, 2003), 71.

to embrace the wide scope of the concept *dikaiosyne* in *one* word. Maybe, then, we should translate it with 'justice-righteousness,' in an attempt to hold on to both dimensions."[283]

The *Theological Wordbook of the Old Testament* (TWOT) offers additional meaning to the definition of *mishpat*: justice, ordinance, custom, manner. This represents what is doubtless the most important idea for correct understanding of government – whether of man by man or of the whole creation by God. Though rendered "judgment" in most of the four hundred or so appearances of *mishpat* in the Hebrew Bible, this rendering is often defective for us moderns by reason of our novel way of distinctly separating legislative, executive, and judicial functions and functionaries in government. Hence *shapat*, the common verb (from which our word *mishpat* is derived) meaning "to rule, govern," referring to all functions of government, is erroneously restricted to judicial processes only, whereas both the verb and noun include all these functions. An analysis of all uses in the Bible turns up at least thirteen related, but distinct, aspects of the central idea, which if to be rendered by a single English word with similar range of meaning, ought by all means to be the word "justice."[284]

Two important observations must be offered regarding TWOT's definition. First, the central idea for the meaning of the word in the English language must be "justice." Secondly, the most common context for the use of the word *mishpat* (justice) is in the context of government. A study of the book of Isaiah reveals that in the overwhelming majority of the texts where *mishpat* (justice) is used, it is referring to the just or unjust manner in which the nation is governed. In almost all of the Messianic passages, the word is used to refer the government of the coming Messiah characterized by justice.

283 Ibid., 71-72.

284 Robert D. Culver, *Theological Wordbook of the Old Testament,* eds. R. Laird Harris, Gleason L. Archer, Jr., and Bruce K. Waltke, (Chicago: Moody Press, 1980), 2:2443-4.

In *Kingdom Ethics,* Glen H. Stassen and David P. Gushee summarize the teaching of Isaiah and Jesus, as he references Isaiah, on social justice with four powerful conclusions. They argue that a careful study of the Scriptures, both Old and New Testaments, reveals the following definition for justice: (1) deliverance of the poor and powerless from the injustice that they regularly experience; (2) lifting the foot of domineering power off the neck of the dominated and oppressed; (3) stopping the violence and establishing peace; and (4) restoring the outcasts, the excluded, the Gentiles, the exiles, and the refugees to community.[285] Stassen and Gushee also suggest that *tsedaqah* means delivering, community-restoring justice, and that *mishpat* means judgment according to right or rights, and thus judgment that vindicates the right especially of the poor or powerless.[286]

In addition, Stassen and Gushee argue that by overlooking the biblical framework and definitions for understanding justice, Christian have allowed secular sources to fill the void and to define justice for us.

> Skipping over the biblical meaning of justice creates a vacuum. In hop secular ideologies, only too happy to fill the vacuum with their justifications of greed, racism or other sinful drives – and only too happy to claim that their ideologies are Christian. The secular ideas of justice that hop in include the Greek aristocratic ethic with its fairly abstract "to everyone his due"; or the thin philosophical concepts of utilitarianism—"the greatest happiness for the greatest number"; or liberalism—"individual autonomy"; or Kant's "treat every person as an end in himself or herself, and never only as a means"; or Rawls's two principles of fairness—"liberty and difference that benefits the least advantaged"; or Walzer's "complex equality" and human rights; the reduction of justice to retribution or punishment; or the drive

285 Glen H. Stassen and David P. Gushee, *Kingdom Ethics: Following Jesus in Contemporary Context* (Downers Grove, IL: InterVarsity Press, 2003), 340.
286 Ibid.

> for political control that reduces justice to "the dictatorship of the proletariat"; or the drive for freedom to pursue wealth that reduces justice to "the dictatorship of the free market." None of these is adequate to communicate the will of God in the biblical teaching of delivering, community-restoring justice and righteousness.[287]

If we are going to understand how the church is to function in relationship to justice, we must extricate it from its captivity to Greek and Western philosophical thought and establish God's mind on justice. How does God think about justice? Stassen and Gushee's argument is that we can get a clear understanding of God's mind on justice not only in the Old Testament but also by examining Jesus' teachings in the gospels. He suggests that Jesus identified, especially strongly, with the tradition of the prophets of Israel. This is clear in the Gospels, and it is clear now in much New Testament scholarship. It was not so clear to previous scholarship influenced by anti-Semitism, by a liberal preference for universal truths rather than the historical particularity of Jesus, and by lack of attention to the historical context of Israel in Jesus' day.

Stassen and Gushee's argument continues with the idea that Jesus' attack on the money changers in the temple was symbolic of an attack in the entire temple system. He argues that:

> Scholars are seeing that it was not merely a "cleansing" of the temple, but a prophetic and symbolic attack on the whole temple system for practicing a cover-up of injustice; the same kind of confrontation offered by both Isaiah 56 and Jeremiah 7. These are the two passages that the Gospels report Jesus quoting when he overturned the tables of the money changers and "would not allow anyone to carry anything through the temple." [288]

287 Ibid., 345-46.
288 Ibid., 347-48.

Gushee's argument suggests that Jesus had a high level of awareness and concern for justice by often citing Old Testament prophets:

> Jesus often cited the prophet Isaiah, which (explicitly in the Aramaic Targum, implicitly but clearly in the Hebrew text) speaks several times of the kingdom or reign of God. This is an important clue for the meaning of the kingdom. In chapter one, we found that sixteen of the seventeen kingdom-deliverance passages in Isaiah announced that justice was a key characteristic of God's kingdom.[289]

Jesus' concern for justice offers an important foundation for the biblical perspective. Jesus, of course, was not captive to Greek philosophical thought. His definition for justice is more in agreement with Bosch's conclusion that the atoning work of the cross is to affect both righteousness in the individual and justice in the community.

### *Reconciliation*

We have seen that Perkins' emphasis on justice has deep biblical roots. However, his concern is not only a concern for justice. It is also a concern for racial reconciliation. John Perkins' model for ministry assumes the deconstruction of racialization by building Christian community with people who have been truly reconciled both to God and to each other.

### *The Argument in Ephesians*

Perkins' assumption of the deconstruction of racialization is implicitly made at several points in his essay, "What is Community Development," in the volume he edited, *Restoring at Risk*

289 Ibid., 348.

*Communities: Doing It Together and Doing It Right.* In this section, I would like to further develop themes Perkins implicitly discusses in order to bring to the fore the way in which his theological assumptions provide a means for dealing not only with racism, but also with racialization. Perkins references the letter to Ephesians, suggesting that each of the first three chapters refer to the idea that the Jewish believing community and the Gentile believing community were required by God to be established as a blended community. In Ephesians, he observes, Paul uses the first three chapters to lay the groundwork for the principle of reconciliation. In chapter 1, Paul tells the Ephesian believers that they are called to bring glory to God. Toward that end, God put into place a divine plan, which Paul calls a "mystery." All things in heaven and earth are to be under one head, even Christ. In chapter 2, Paul talks about how God has brought those who were formerly alienated together into one body. Again, it is presented as a major, long-term plan by God: "His purpose was to create in himself one new man out of the two, thus making peace, and in this one body to reconcile both of them to God through the cross, by which he put to death their hostility" (vv. 15-16, NIV). Then in chapter 3, Paul brings up the "mystery" again, this eternal plan to sum up all creation under one head: "This mystery is that through the gospel the Gentiles are heirs together with Israel, members together of one body, and sharers together in the promise in Christ Jesus" (v. 6, NIV).[290]

Perkins suggests that racial segregation is not compatible with Paul's theology: "There was no room in Paul's gospel for theological or racial division...It is clear that the message of reconciliation between Jew and Gentile was a central part of the gospel Paul preached."[291] He also refuses to embrace a racialized worldview by

290 John M. Perkins, *Restoring At-Risk Communities: Doing It Together and Doing It Right* (Grand Rapids: Baker Books, 1995), 32.
291 Ibid.

suggesting that racial and ethnic barriers are man-made, "A gospel that could not reconcile humans across the most difficult barrier of the day was no gospel at all. So it is with us. If the gospel is not concerned with reconciling us across the most stubborn ethnic and racial, indeed, all man-made barriers, then it is no gospel at all."[292]

Paul's argument that the social stratification resulting from racialization must be deconstructed is even stronger than the brief argument outlined in the Perkins' material. Paul teaches that the identities created by the social and political systems of the first century must be eliminated and replaced by identities consistent with sonship. One of the major themes in the first two chapters of Paul's letter to the Ephesians is the requirement of God for believing Jews and believing Gentiles to be blended into one family. Stated earlier, this is an argument for integration but Paul takes it farther. After drawing a brief picture of the integration of believing Jews and believing Gentiles, Paul uses language that begins to frame the requirements for successful reconciliation.

Paul launches into a description of family relationship and a unity that can happen only if the two groups have experienced total reconciliation. The Jewish and Gentile relationship can no longer exist as "tolerated neighbors" or as "guests in the owner's house," the Gentile living in a subordinate relationship with the superior Jewish community. Richard Lenski observes that once the Gentiles were "foreigners" (v. 12), that is, aliens and strangers. They were "guests" in the nation or the city to which they had come for a shorter or a longer stay. As such, they only were tolerated. Paul adds to this the idea that the synonymous "outsiders" (*paroikoi;* literally, living beside each other, v. 19), were also tolerated neighbors and no more. The outsider was "a licensed sojourner in a town, whose protection and status were secured by the payment of a small tax."

292 Ibid., 33.

Lenski points to an "inscription which shows the mixed nature of the population in Graeco-Roman towns." He concludes that in this mix a *xenos* might be a mere traveler; a *paroikos* was one who dwelt in a city that was not of his own people.[293]

Skevington Wood adds interesting commentary on the same verses. Using a formula he is especially fond of ("consequently," *ara oun*, v. 19), Paul draws a conclusion from the previous paragraph (vv.14-18). Verses 19-22 represent a further expansion of verse 13. Two technical terms commonly denoting inferiority of status are contrasted with *sympolitai* ("fellow citizens"). The first (*xenoi*) applies to "foreigners" in general but in particular to short-term transients. The other (*paroikoi*) were the resident "aliens" who had settled in the country of their choice. The *paroikos* was "a licensed sojourner in a town whose protection and status were secured by the payment of a small tax." He had no intrinsic rights, however. Such had been the position of the Gentiles in relation to the kingdom of God before the coming of Christ. But now they enjoy all the privileges of God's new people. They are united with the saints of the past (Eph. 1:18) as well as with contemporary Christians. This togetherness is stressed again in verses 21 and 22. The Gentiles are not only *sympolitai* but *oikeioi tou theou*, "members of God's household." Wycliffe has "household men of God." As Abbott explained, the phrase describes the theocracy in its domestic aspect.[294]

*The NIV Study Bible*, with notes on Ephesians by Walter L. Liefeld, comments on verse 19. The Gentiles at Ephesus are particularly in mind here with the use of the terms "citizens" and "household." This is familiar imagery. The household in ancient times was what we today might call an extended family. Paul is teaching that these two

293 R. C. H. Lenski, *The Interpretation of St. Paul's Epistles to Galatians, Ephesians and Philippians* (Minneapolis, MN: Augsburg, 1937), 449.

294 A. Skevington Wood, "Ephesians," in *The Expositor's Bible Commentary: Ephesians through Philemon*, ed. Frank E. Gaebelein (Grand Rapids: Zondervan, 1978), 11:41.

groups, who for centuries had been mortal enemies, have to live together as brothers in the same family. They are now to be fellow-citizens in the same house, living together as equal partners. [295]

Although Paul's references cannot be said to be referring directly to racial issues, but to ethnocentrism, the first cousin to racism, the stratification experienced in the community of believers was not to be tolerated. The newcomers to the community were to be given follow-citizen status and equally privileged as the original members.

### *Paul's Struggle with the Judaizers*

The apostle Paul's theology presents his Jewish ethnic identity as not only valid but also as something that he honors and values. However, in a tricky balance Paul stops short of validating ethnocentrism. One of the difficult tensions faced by the apostle in his home church in Antioch was the struggle with the Judaizers. Judaizers are likely Christians who had come out of Pharisaism. On the surface, it appears that the problem of the Judaizers in Galatia was theological, a problem with legalism. However, a closer examination reveals that the problem was really the sin of ethnocentrism. The text shows ethnocentrism as a problem with not only the Judaizers but also a problem for Peter. The argument begins with Peter's visit to Simon of Joppa's house in Acts 10. His response to the Lord's suggestion to eat unclean foods was met with a refusal to act contrary to the Mosaic law codes about food. However, God convinced Peter that the food was no longer unclean. God had made it clean. The next day Peter entered the house of Cornelius, a Gentile centurion, and announced (v. 28) his belief that it was unlawful

295 Walter L. Liefeld, "Notes on Ephesians," *The NIV Study Bible: New International Version,* ed. Kenneth L. Barker (Grand Rapids: Zondervan, 1985), 1793.

for him, a Jew, to *kollasthai* (associate, or join closely together)[296] or to *proserxesthai* (visit or approach)[297] an *allophulō* (foreigner or heathen).[298] Paul uses a very specific word, meaning "one of another nation," in this verse only used twice in the New Testament. It is not the common word *ethnos* used for a Gentile or the nations. Thayer suggests that *allophulō* is a person who is not a Jew. He suggests that it comes from a combination of *allos* (another) and *phulon* (tribe). It would then mean anyone who comes from a tribe other that the twelve tribes of Jacob. Peter follows his announcement by saying that God had told him not to call "any man" (*anthrōpon*, literally, a human being) unclean or common. Peter's ethnocentrism had been exposed. God taught him that Jews, as men, are no better than men from other tribes. Peter then shared the gospel with Cornelius, his friends, and his relatives. The Gentiles received the Holy Spirit as evidence that God was including the gentiles in this new community of his people as well as the Jews. The story picks up in chapter 11 with Peter, now in Jerusalem, being challenged by the circumcision party for eating with Gentiles (vv. 1-3). In the following verses (4-17), Peter explains in detail what he had experienced in Joppa and in Cornelius' house. Uncircumcised Gentiles had heard the gospel, believed, and received the Holy Spirit. Verse 18 says Peter's challengers ended their critical remarks and admitted that God was doing something different. He was now giving Gentiles repentance and life. Chapter 15 has Peter, as the head of the church in Jerusalem, making a decision, in opposition to the believers who had been Pharisees, to accept Gentiles into the church without requiring them to first be circumcised. Then, Galatians 2 has Peter in Antioch eating with Gentiles. This has to have taken place after Peter's Joppa and Jerusalem counsel experience (Acts 15). Peter was

296 F. Wilbur Gingrich, *Shorter Lexicon of the Greek New Testament* (Chicago: University of Chicago Press, 1971), 118.
297 Ibid., 185-186.
298 Ibid., 10.

doing something that he confessed to God (Acts 10:14) that he had never done, namely eat unclean food. Peter was also associating with uncircumcised Gentile believers, something that had been clarified at the Jerusalem Counsel in Acts 15. Galatians 2:12 records Peter again being challenged by Judaizers about his relationship with Gentiles. This time Peter acquiesced and withdrew from his Gentile friends. Craig Keener's comments are insightful here:

> The Jerusalem Jewish leaders may have agreed with Paul on paper (in theory), but they also had to keep peace within their own Jerusalem constituency and maintain their witness to their culture, with its rising anti-Gentile sentiments. Peter probably saw his own actions here the way Paul saw his own in 1 Corinthians 9:19-22 – appealing to everyone – but the qualitative difference is enormous: withdrawing from table fellowship with culturally different Christians made them second – class citizens, violated the unity of the church and hence insulted the cross of Christ. Although Peter and others undoubtedly claimed to oppose racism, they accommodated it on what they saw as minor points to keep peace, whereas Paul felt that any degree of racial separatism or segregation challenged the heart of the gospel.[299]

When the men from James came to Antioch, all of the Jews, including Peter and Barnabas, got caught up in what Keener calls racism. It may be more accurate to identify the problem as ethnocentrism. Classic social political categories normally associated with race were yet to be developed. However, tribal, ethnic, and national categories were fully developed since the Tower in Genesis 11 and ethnic superiority was clearly being employed in Antioch by the Jews. The apostle Paul, who was also in Antioch at the time, challenged the Jews and Peter for their hypocrisy.

299 Craig S. Keener, *The IVP Bible Background Commentary: New Testament* (Downers Grove, IL: InterVarsity Press, 1993), 523.

Immediately after challenging Peter for his expression of ethnic superiority, Paul makes a statement that almost validates the actions of the Judaizers. Paul acknowledges the ethnic distinctiveness of the Jewish people compared to Gentile people: "We ourselves are Jews by birth and not Gentile sinners" (Gal. 2:20). Paul uses the same word that he used in Ephesians 2:3, *physis*, here translated in the *English Standard Version* as "by birth," with Colin Brown offering the meaning descent or extraction.[300] In Ephesians, the descendants come from Adam, here, the descendants come from Jewish tribes.

Paul almost acquiesces to the sins of bias being expressed by Peter, the men from James, and the rest of the Jews. However, his position is clarified in Galatians 2:20. He says, "and the life I now live in the flesh I live by faith in the Son of God." Paul is saying the life that he lived as an ethnic Jew is trumped by the cross. So his ethnic heritage is maintained as valuable but not to the point where it cause him to commit the sin of ethnocentrism.

### *Sin as a Loss of Sonship*

What are the direct implications of the fall of Adam into sin? There are two. Adam acquired personal guilt. Romans 5:12 says, "Therefore, just as sin came into the world through one man, and death through sin, and so death spread to all men because all sinned." What is death? Death is what God promised would happen to Adam if he disobeyed God. Death is what happened to Adam as he and Eve eat the fruit. Death is broken fellowship with God. However, death is not only limited to Adam, it was also imputed to every human being in the loins of Adam so each individual human acquired not only personal guilt but an insatiable drive to compensate for this loss.

300 Gunther Harder, *The International Dictionary of New Testament Theology*, ed. Colin Brown (Grand Rapids: Zondervan, 1976), 2:660.

This drive has led to the development of collective compensatory sources of identity.

As a modern ideology, racialization became a dominant component of Western worldview shortly after the Enlightenment. Although there have been forms of cultural prejudice since the Garden of Eden, classic racism developed in conjunction with racialization. Although these ideas are late developments, the roots of ethnocentrism, racialization and racism can be traced back to the Tower of Babel, with seeds found in the assault on Adam's identity by Satan in Genesis 3. After creating man in his own image and placing him in the garden, God's intention, revealed in Genesis 1:28, has been to glorify himself by filling the earth with his own image. The best science suggests that human variation has resulted from the natural selection of genes that pooled in accord with geographic distance one group from another. In an interview for the documentary *Race: The Power of an Illusion,* Joseph Graves says:

> The best way to understand the genetic differences that we find in human populations is that populations differ by distance. And so populations that are closer to each other geographically are more likely to share common gene variants, whereas populations that are further apart are going to share fewer genes. Human populations differ in gene frequencies relative to their geographic location. And it's a continuous change from one group to another... if we were to walk from the tropics to the Norway, what we would see is a continuous change in skin tone. And at no point along that trip would we be able to say, "Oh, this is the place in which we go from the dark race to the light race."[301]

301 PBS. *Race: The Power of an Illusion*. PBS. Interview with Joseph Graves, Jr. Executive producer Larry Adelman. California Newsreel: 2003. http://www.pbs.org/race000 About/002 o4-background-01006.htm (accessed March 13, 2009).

Graves' observations are consistent with the biblical account: "So the LORD dispersed them from there over the face of all the earth, and they left off building the city. Therefore its name was called Babel, because there the LORD confused the language of all the earth. And from there the LORD dispersed them over the face of all the earth" (Gen. 11:8-9).

Therefore, because of language imputed by the LORD, man, in his confusion, migrated in language groups from Shinar to every corner of the earth. As man migrated, their cultural expression changed driven by available resources and climate. Skin tone changed in accord with the amount of available sunlight. Assuming God's intention for self-glorification, his plan to saturate the earth with his image, as well as human variation resulting from geographic location on the earth, leads to the conclusion that human variation does not diminish the image of God in man. Keil and Delitzsch draw the same conclusion: For, according to the divine purpose, men were to fill the earth, i.e. to spread over the whole earth, not indeed to separate, but to maintain their inward unity notwithstanding their dispersion.[302] Even if the fall never took place nor the necessity for God's intervention at the Tower, man would have filled the earth, human variation would have still developed based on God's design, and God would still have maintained His glory over all the earth through mankind.

Human variation does not change man's ability to glorify God because it has not resulted in a change in human ontology. However, mankind did change in the nature of his experiential knowledge of good and evil as the result of his disobedience recorded in Genesis 3. The text records Satan saying that eating the forbidden fruit would result in a fundamental change in the nature of man's soul. The lie,

302 C. F. Keil and F. Delitzsch, *Commentary on the Old Testament*, 10 vols. (Grand Rapids: Eerdmans, 1976), 1:173.

"you will not surely die," was mixed with the truth "you will be like God, knowing good and evil." The Hebrew word in Genesis 3:5 translated "you will be" comes from the root word *hyh*. The verb form is a second person plural masculine preterite. The word means "to be, become, to exist or to become like."[303] In this case, Adam and Eve became like God. This idea finds emphasis with the preposition *k*, which means "as, like, the like of,"[304] used as a prefix on the word *elohim*. This idea, becoming like God, knowing good and evil is repeated in verse 22. However, in addition to the two propositional statements, one a lie and the other a partial truth, there is a third unspoken propositional statement. In addition to becoming like God, Adam and Eve also became like "the father of lies," Satan (cf. John 8:44). It is here that a major shift in identity takes place. Adam and Eve are no longer sons of God but are now "sons of disobedience," the identity given by Paul in Ephesians 2:2. They are now identified, by the apostle, as followers of the prince of the power of the air. Jesus identifies those who follow Satan to be "of your father the devil, and your will is to do your father's desires. He was a murderer from the beginning, and has nothing to do with the truth" (John 8:44). Further support for the notion that an identity change had taken place is found in Ephesians 2:3. Paul claims that both Jew and Gentiles were at one time "by nature children of wrath." Post Adamic man stands in opposition to God and under the judgment of God's wrath. The word *physis* is translated nature. Colin Brown offers the meaning descent or extraction.[305] The heathen are as sinners and as transgressors of the first commandment by nature, by descent. Who are they descendent from? The answer has to be Adam. So as Adam was a follower of Satan and became a child of the Devil so is the unregenerate sinner.

303 Victor P. Hamilton, *Theological Wordbook of the Old Testament*, 1:213.
304 John N. Oswalt, *Theological Wordbook of the Old Testament*, 1:425.
305 Harder, *The International Dictionary of New Testament Theology*, 2:660.

Adam's son Cain exemplifies the loss of a son relationship to God the Father. After murdering his brother Able, God's curse on Cain included not having access to the garden or the tree of life, the ground will no longer yield fruit for him, and he is identified as a "fugitive and a wanderer on the earth" (Gen. 4:12). Both Hebrew words translated "fugitive" *(nua)* and "wanderer" (*nod*) carry the meaning of "a wandering people on a geographic scale, homeless vagabonds who are outside the protection of the law or of any fixed social group."[306] As sons of disobedience and sons of the Devil, mankind has no sense of identity, no connection to a people, no place to call home.[307] With the relationship to the Creator broken, and his purpose to glorify God disrupted, mankind has no sense of purpose. Even after the flood, Noah's sons were wanderers. The Tower of Babel event brings the situation to a head. Then they said, "Come, let us build ourselves a city and a tower, with its top in the heavens, and let us make a name for ourselves, lest we be dispersed over the face of the whole earth" (Gen. 11:4). However, God's intervention dispersed man, through the imputation of language, resulting in the first reference, Genesis 10, to the development of both ethnic and national identities. Genesis 10 records the first uses of both terms *gohy* translated "nation" and *mishpaha* translated "clan." R. Laird Harris translates *gohy* as "people" or "nation," or simply as a "defined body or group of people."[308] Hermann J. Austel translates *mishpaha* as a "circle of relatives with strong blood ties."[309] The word *goy* is used at least 500 times and the word *mishpaha* is used at least 250 times in the rest of the Old Testament. Human wandering and seeking for a compensatory identity, after the loss of the son relationship to God the Father, took firm root in ethnic and national sources.

---

306 Andrew Bowling, *Theological Wordbook of the Old Testament*, 2:564.
307 Ibid.
308 Gerard Van Groningen, *Theological Wordbook of the Old* Testament, 1:153.
309 Hermann J. Austel, *Theological Wordbook of the Old Testament*, 2:947.

The gospel addresses the problem of sin, which at its root is a loss of a relationship with the creator, the Father of all humankind. The loss of our true identity in relation the Father leads us to seek compensatory identities, such as those given to us by our race, class, or ethnicity. Paul's theology addresses this difficulty. Christ's death and resurrection offers the promise given to Abraham to all people (Gal. 3:13-14). The cultural cosmos of the ancient world – founded as it was on fundamental distinctions (e.g., between male and female, Jew and Greek, slave and free) – no longer exists for those baptized into Christ's death and resurrection (Gal. 3:28).[310] For Paul, justification by faith has to do with our adoption as heirs to the promise Abraham received by faith, a promise of descendants and progeny that would culminate in the sending of the Spirit.[311] We no longer need to rely on compensatory identities. The barriers among us have been broken down. The atonement, Jesus' death for humanity's sin, provides a new basis for approaching race relationships. A new people now exists, whose old identities have been crucified with Christ and whose new selves are now enacted solely by faith in Christ (Gal. 2:20). Through the Spirit, old distinctions no longer count – even the most fundamental distinction between who is righteous and who is not – all that counts now is "faith working through love" (Gal. 5:6). The same Spirit who raised Jesus from the dead has been given to us, enabling us to put on as our own, Christ's identity as the beloved child of God (Rom. 8:9-17). By faith in Christ, we now share Jesus' identity as the beloved child of God; we need no longer by enslaved by fear. The powers and forces of this passing age no longer have control over us. We have received the Spirit and through the Spirit we not only experience the intimacy Jesus had with his "Abba" (Gal. 4:6; Rom. 8:15-16), but we are also transformed into Christ's image

310 See, e.g., J. Louis Martyn, "Apocalyptic Antinomies in Paul's Letter to the Galatians," *New Testament Studies* 31 (1985), 424.

311 See Rom. 3:27-4:25 and Gal. 3:6-14; cf. Gen. 12-17.

(2 Cor. 3:18). As we enter more fully into this new identity, we have a new basis for relating to one another (Gal. 5).

In sum, the gospel deals not only with the problem of racism, but with the deeper problem of racialization, the deeper problem of our defining the core of our identities in terms of the categories of race. The gospel not only deals with sin, but grants a new identity, one based on sonship through Jesus. The gospel creates a new identity and this establishes a basis for not only addressing racism, but racialization as well. Instead of merely darning ourselves in terms of our families of origin, as the pictures that follow point out, we now have a new basis for identity.

This is reconciliation. This tense relationship between the believing Jews and Gentiles in the first century has many parallels in the social landscape of the United States of America over the past 150 years. The freedom of the African from American enslavement in 1863 and 1865 mandated that white Americans and the new black Americans become one American nation. It is this mandate that Booker T. Washington, W.E.B. DuBois, James Cone, Gayraud Wilmore, J. Deotis Roberts, and John Perkins have been working to achieve.

In their book *Divided by Faith,* Michael Emerson and Christian Smith describe the society of the United States as being racialized: "A racialized society is a society wherein race matters profoundly for differences in life experiences, life opportunities, and social relationships. A racialized society can also be said to be a 'society that allocates differential economic, political, social, and even psychological rewards to groups along racial lines; lines that are socially constructed."[312] Emerson and Smith use the word to describe a society without really defining it. In doing so, they do not make enough distinction between the meaning of *racism* and what is

312 Michael O. Emerson and Christian Smith, *Divided by Faith: Evangelical Relations and the Problem of Race in America*, (New York: Oxford Press, 2001), 7.

meant by a *racialized society.* It is important to make a cleaner distinction between the meanings of the two words. Racialization is a worldview and racism is the by-product of this worldview. The distinction has important implications for any group in society that is trying to address the issues. The problem of definitions has specific application in any attempt to bring solution. The society that is attempting to effect justice must deconstruct the worldview of racialization. Its people must cease to think through a racial frame of reference. However, deconstructing racialization leaves the task only half completed. Justice also requires that the society undo and reverse the effects of a racialized and racist system.

Compensatory identities based on race and ethnicities have filled the void of this lost sonship. These compensating sources of identity correspond with the racial typological categories, Negroid, Caucasoid, and Mongoloid among many others. Working within compensatory identities limits the progress that can be made in reducing the effects of racialization because the players are always caught in a "them and us matrix." This "them and us matrix" will maintain the competition noted by Shelby Steele, where the races are constantly "fighting for innocence."[313]

Perkins' biblical model not only addresses racism by depersonalizing it, but it also positions the church to address ethnocentrism. By draining racialization of power, Perkins' model is able to embrace the balance taught by the apostle Paul validating ethnic and cultural distinctiveness, while offering spiritual maturity as the solution for the sins that are ethnocentric in emphasis. Models that are black or white, trapped within the racial matrix, cannot offer this kind of balance. They are, in fact, ethnocentric in nature themselves. John Perkins' conservative perspective on the Scripture

313 Shelby Steele, *The Contents of Our Character: A New Vision of Race in America* (New York: Harper Collins, 1991), 11.

and conservative theology offer sonship as an identity category and a way out of the racial matrix. His position on the historicity of Scripture, the Genesis account in particular, also allows him to take spiritual warfare seriously. Satan, understood as a personal being and the father of lies, told the two greatest lies in human history. These remain lies that hold humanity hostage. The first was "you will not surely die." The second, developed over a period of several hundred years, was that race is biologically based. Perkins' Christ-centered, spiritually based model answers these two lies and stands as the new paradigm for building Christian community against the old paradigm that is being informed by a racialized worldview.

## A RESPONSE TO AN OBJECTION

In *Divided by Faith*, Emerson and Smith argued that much of the racial dysfunction in the American church today is the result of an individualized theological worldview that blinds white evangelicals to certain societal injustices.[314] The book's thesis created much debate among many evangelical leaders. Three years later, Emerson teamed with fellow sociologists Karen Chai Kim and George Yancey and with theologian Curtiss Paul DeYoung to write a sequel, *United by Faith: The Multiracial Congregation as an Answer to the Problem of Race*.[315] The team – who define a multiracial church as "a congregation in which no one racial group accounts for 80 percent or more of the membership" – did an intensive, three-year study that included 2,500 phone interviews, written surveys taken by 500 congregations, and firsthand observations of churches in four diverse metropolitan areas. The authors provided yet another

314 Emerson and Smith, *Divided by Faith*.

315 Curtiss Paul DeYoung et al., *United by Faith: The Multiracial Congregation As an Answer to the Problem of Race* (New York: Oxford University Press, 2004).

compelling challenge, and intensified their call, which they argue is a biblical one, for more churches to become multiracial.

The authors argued that the nation's racial landscape is changing. According to the 2000 Census, people of color as a percentage of the United States population have *more than doubled* to 31 percent since 1960, and the growth of non-Europeans is expected to continue at an accelerated rate. In just the last 20 years (1980 to 2000), the African American population grew by nearly 30 percent, the Native American population by 75 percent, the Latino population by 142 percent, and the Asian American population by 185 percent. In absolute numbers, the United States had well over 35 million *more* people of color in 2000 than it did in 1980. This is more people than lived in the entire United States during the Civil War period of the early 1860s.

Race, as it always has, plays a significant part in the lives of people living in the United States. As the authors maintain, "it shapes where people live and whom they live with, where people send their children to school, with whom they can most easily become friends, their likelihood of having access to wealth and health, whom they marry, how they think about themselves, and their cultural tastes."[316] Race also shapes how people value others, how much they trust others, provides quick stereotypes by which to classify people, and shapes fears of crime. As Cornel West succinctly puts it, "Race matters."

Where one worships can be correlated with race. Congregations have long been highly racially segregated. The authors maintain that if we define a racially mixed congregation as one in which no one racial group is 80 percent or more of the congregation, just 7.5 percent of the more than 300,000 religious congregations in

316 Curtiss Paul DeYoung et al., "All Churches Should be Multiracial: The Biblical Case," ChrTo, 1 April 2005, http://www.christianitytoday .com/ct/2005/april/22.33.html (accessed November 30, 2009).

the United States are racially mixed. For Christian congregations, which form more than 90 percent of congregations in the United States, the share that is racially mixed drops to 5.5 percent. Of this small percentage, approximately half of the congregations are mixed only temporarily, during the time they are in transition from one group to another.[317]

This book sets out to make a bold, clear, controversial argument: "Christian congregations, when possible, should be multiracial." They call for "the emergence of a movement toward more multiracial congregations" and argue that the twenty-first century must be "the century of multiracial congregations." Their conclusion rests in part on the premise that multiracial congregations can play an important role in reducing racial division and inequality and that this should be a goal of Christian people. The authors argue that the future of Christianity in the twenty-first century depends on "practical, living examples of authentic reconciling faith." Although they acknowledge that "multiracial congregations will never be perfect organizations," they nonetheless maintain that "God's call to reconciliation through the life, death, and resurrection and abiding presence of Jesus Christ compels us to embrace the challenge of moving forward toward this goal."[318]

Paul Helseth, John Piper and Jarvis Williams are three evangelical theologians with hearts for racial justice. Each has done honorable theological work to support justice. However John Perkins' insistence on intentionality exposes differences in some of the theological and sociological assumptions that need to be addressed if the church is going to move beyond social integration toward true biblical reconciliation.

---

317 Ibid.
318 Ibid.

In his article "Elect from Every Nation: Racial Reconciliation Won't Happen If We Don't Take Ephesians Seriously" published in Touchstone, Helseth articulates some of the most important objections held by many white evangelical and fundamentalist Christians to John Perkins' approach to race relations. Helseth's objection to the notions of collective identity and collective guilt is well taken when guilt is assessed simply because of one's membership in groups identified as "White, Western and Wealthy."[319]

However these are social political constructs. They are not individual people. Guilt can be accurately laid at the feet of whiteness (the social construct), Western ethnocentrism, and materialism. Culpability is assessed to individuals only when individuals or organizations behave in ways that are complicit with the sins of these political constructs. In the church, these constructs maintain the potential to supplant our identities as children of God with the propensity for members to behave with complicity to the sin patterns and policies of the collective. Perkins' model of de-racialization resolves this tension by disconnecting the social political construct from individual people, leaving all of us free to attack the distortions in society created by the constructs. Christ has removed our objective estrangement from him. By removing this estrangement and making us children of God, Christ has established the platform for the deconstruction of the source of alienation brother from brother and sister from sister based on perceived racial differences.

As important as this discussion is, the core of Helseth's arguments is grounded in his interpretation of Ephesians 2 a interpretation consistent with the traditional Evangelical understanding of Ephesians 2 and is similar, if not identical, to

319 Paul Kjoss Helseth et al., "Elect from Every Nation: Racial Reconciliation Won't Happen If We Don't Take Ephesians Seriously," Touchstone, September 2007, http://www.touchstonemag.com/archives/article.php?id=20-07-026-f (accessed November 30, 2009).

both Piper and Williams understanding of the Apostle Paul's teaching in this text.

> In Ephesians Paul speaks of what God accomplished on the Cross as an established reality (2:11–22). Through the Cross, God reconciled believers to himself and to one another by creating "one new man" in Christ Jesus. According to Paul, we are now at peace with God and with each other because Christ abolished "in his flesh" the "enmity" that separated us from his Father and from one another. But what was this "enmity" that Christ abolished? Paul explains that it was the "law of commandments and ordinances" that excluded Gentiles from "the commonwealth of Israel" and "the covenants of promise," and which itself was the basis for racial alienation in the Old Testament. His point is simply that Christ has already reconciled believers to God and to one another by removing the objective source of their estrangement. From this it follows that those who are in the "one new man" by faith are now unified and members of the same "household of God," and that the reluctance to acknowledge this reality calls the redemptive historical significance of the Cross into question. [320]

Horizontal and vertical reconciliation taking place simultaneously between the believer and God and the believer and his or believing neighbor is a well accepted view of Ephesians 2:14-17 among a majority of Evangelicals. John Piper makes virtually the same claim in his excellent book *Blood Lines*.

> THE RABBI WAS MISTAKEN
>
> There are not two saving covenants. There are not two saved peoples. And the reason is that there are not two ways of salvation. There are not two Saviors or two crosses. What could be clearer than this: "[Christ] has broken down

320 Ibid.

> in his flesh the dividing wall of hostility … that he …. might reconcile us both to God in one body through the cross" (Eph. 2:14–16). Jew and Gentile are reconciled to each other by being reconciled to God "through the cross." One way to God for both of us, not two ways. And we go together, or not at all. So there is one saving covenant, the new covenant in the blood of Christ. In believing on Christ, we are reconciled to God. And in being both reconciled to God through Christ, we are reconciled to each other. There is no clearer text in the Bible, it seems to me, than verse 16, concerning the indivisibility of reconciliation to God through the death of Christ and reconciliation to each other of all people groups who come to God through Christ. Vertical and horizontal reconciliation happen together and inseparably through faith in Christ. [321]

This line of exegetical reasoning makes a number of theological assumptions about what Paul is saying in this text and offers several inadequate, though traditional, answers for questions presented by the text. It is in Jarvis Williams' excellent work entitled *One New Man* that the most detailed exposition is offered and the theological assumptions are presented. Williams states in this quote: "Ephesians 2:16 is the key verse of my thesis:"

> With reconciliation in view, Eph 2:15–16 is quite amazing for at least two reasons: (1) Paul uses violent, warlike language (destruction, death through a cross, and the killing of enmity) to describe the hostility that existed between Jews and Gentiles and the peace Jesus achieved for them, and (2) he states that both Jews and Gentiles were reconciled to God through Jesus' cross. Ephesians 2:16 is the key verse of my thesis: Jesus' death is the foundation of Paul's theology of racial reconciliation. Paul does not state here that Jesus' death hypothetically achieved or can possibly assist in the endeavor of reconciliation between Jews and Gentiles.60 Instead, he

321 Piper, John (2011-09-06). *Blood Lines* (Kindle Locations 1828-1844). Good News Publishers. Kindle Edition.

> emphatically states that Jesus' death has accomplished it for the believing community of faith (see 1:15; 2:8–9)! [322]

With Ephesians 2:16 at the center of the argument, what is Paul saying and how does what he is saying fit into the overall argument? Is the phrase "reconcile us both to God in one body" a soteriological statement or an eschatological statement? Do circumcision and the Mosaic Law standing between the Jews and Gentiles creating hostility create hostility among the Gentiles ethnic groups as well? Does removing the source of hostility (circumcision and the Mosaic Law) between the Jews and the Gentiles dissipate the hostility among the Gentiles ethnic groups? Does the becoming one body take place after the reconciliation of both to God? With a close study of Ephesians 2:11-16 questions 2,3 and 4 must be answered no and the phrase "reconcile us both to God" must be understood eschatologically and not soteriologically. We also have to conclude that removing the source of hostility between the Jews and the Gentiles does clarify that each must come to God the same way by faith however there is still more to do if harmony is going to be established among the nations (ethnic groups). So vertical and horizontal reconciliation are not complete and do not take place because we are all in the same covenant community.

Williams draws some excellent conclusions in the last chapter of his book. "Ethnic diversity is not racial reconciliation. Ethnic diversity is not enough." But the chapter also reveals that more theological work needs to be done.

> According to Paul, racial reconciliation suggests that because of Jesus' death for humanity's sin, Jews and Gentiles who have faith in Christ are recreated into one new man. From Paul's perspective racial reconciliation expresses that the

322 Williams, Jarvis (2010-10-01). *One New Man: The Cross and Racial Reconciliation in Pauline Theology* (Kindle Locations 3299-3302). B&H Publishing. Kindle Edition.

> boundary markers once separating Jews and Gentiles from one another do not matter anymore because Christ's death destroyed them. That Gentiles are not circumcised does not matter anymore. That Jews are circumcised does not matter anymore. That Caucasians and Africans enslaved Africans does not matter anymore. [323]

The question this conclusion leaves us with is how has circumcision ever affected the relationship between Caucasians and Africans unless they were proselytes to Judaism? Williams goes on to suggest:

> … Ethnic diversity only means that people from various backgrounds worship, work, or live in the same environment. To the contrary, racial reconciliation means that different races are now members of the same spiritual family by their faith in Christ because of his death for sin, and they have equal access to God by the same Spirit since Jesus recreated all who believe into one new man. This new man is the new race in Christ. This new race transcends our old ethnic identities and our old man in Adam (see Rom 6:6). [324]

Theologically as well as socially Williams definitions of ethnic diversity and racial reconciliation end up meaning the same thing. People from various backgrounds sharing worship, work, living space, family and can be identified as Christians together. These are simply definitions of social integration. The last phrase reveals where the work must continue. What does it mean to have new identities and what does in mean to be "in Christ?"

The church of Jesus Christ has seen significant change in the area of race relations since the 1960s. Christians have become convinced that racism is sin requiring a change in the ways we do

323 Williams, Jarvis (2010-10-01). *One New Man: The Cross and Racial Reconciliation in Pauline Theology* (Kindle Locations 3618-3619). B&H Publishing. Kindle Edition.

324 Williams, Jarvis (2010-10-01). *One New Man: The Cross and Racial Reconciliation in Pauline Theology* (Kindle Locations 3621-3624). B&H Publishing. Kindle Edition.

church and the ways in which we related to one another. However, the changes are superficial and incomplete expressly because the church still supports a racialized worldview. The ministry of Dr. John M. Perkins offers hope that we can overcome racialization. Addressing racialization is not an inexpensive task; it will take a monumental commitment to spiritual growth and biblical integrity. Most of all it will require that we all are willing to die to self.

# BIBLIOGRAPHY

Amjad-Ali, Charles and W. Alvin Pitcher, eds. *Liberation and Ethics*. Chicago: Center for the Scientific Study of Religion, 1985.

Anderson, Victor. Beyond Ontological Blackness: An Assay on African American Religious and Cultural Criticism. New York: Continuum, 1995.

Aristotle. *The Politics*. Translated by Carnes Lord. Chicago: The University of Chicago Press, 1984.

Bartkoski, John and Helen Regis. *Charitable Choices: Religion, Race, and Poverty in the Post-Welfare Era*. New York: New York University Press, 2003.

Bayor, Ronald H. The Columbia Documentary History of Race and Ethnicity in America. New York: Columbia University Press, 2004.

Beach, Waldo and H. Richard Niebuhr. *Christian Ethics: Sources of the Living Tradition*. New York: The Ronald Press, 1955.

Bender, Kimlyn J. *Karl Barth's Christological Ecclesiology*. Burlington: Ashgate Publishers, 2005.

Bennett, John B. *Christian Ethics and Social Policy*. New York: Scribner's Sons, 1946.

Berk, Stephen. *A Time to Heal*. Grand Rapids: Baker Books, 1997.

Betsworth, Roger G. *Social Ethics: An Examination of American Moral Traditions*. Louisville: Westminster/John Knox Press, 1990.

"Black Enrollments at Christian Colleges Are on the Rise." *The Journal of Blacks in Higher Education* (August 7, 2008). http://www.jbhe.com (accessed January 13, 2009).

Bloom, Herold. *W.E.B. DuBois (Bloom's Modern Critical Views)*. Philadelphia: Chelsea House Publishers, 2003.

Bonhoeffer, Dietrich. *Ethics*. London: SCM Press, 1955.

———. *Sanctorum Communio: A Theological Study of the Sociology of the Church*. Minneapolis: Fortress Press, 1998.

Bosch, David J. *Transforming Mission*. New York: Orbis, 1972.

California Newsreel. *Race: The Power of an Illusion*. DVD transcripts. Larry Adelman, executive producer. 2003. http://www.newsreel.org/transcripts/ race2.htm (accessed August 8, 2008).

Caneday, A. B. "In the Name of the Father, the Son, and the Spirit of Diversity: Multiculturalism Goes to College." *Christian Research Institute* 3, no. 2 (2007).

Cone, James H. *Black Theology and Black Power*. New York: Orbis Books, 1999.

———. *A Black Theology of Liberation*. 20th anniversary ed. New York: Orbis Books, 1990.

———. *For My People: Black Theology and the Black Church*. New York: Orbis Books, 1984.

———. *God of the Oppressed*. Rev. ed. New York: Orbis Books, 1997.

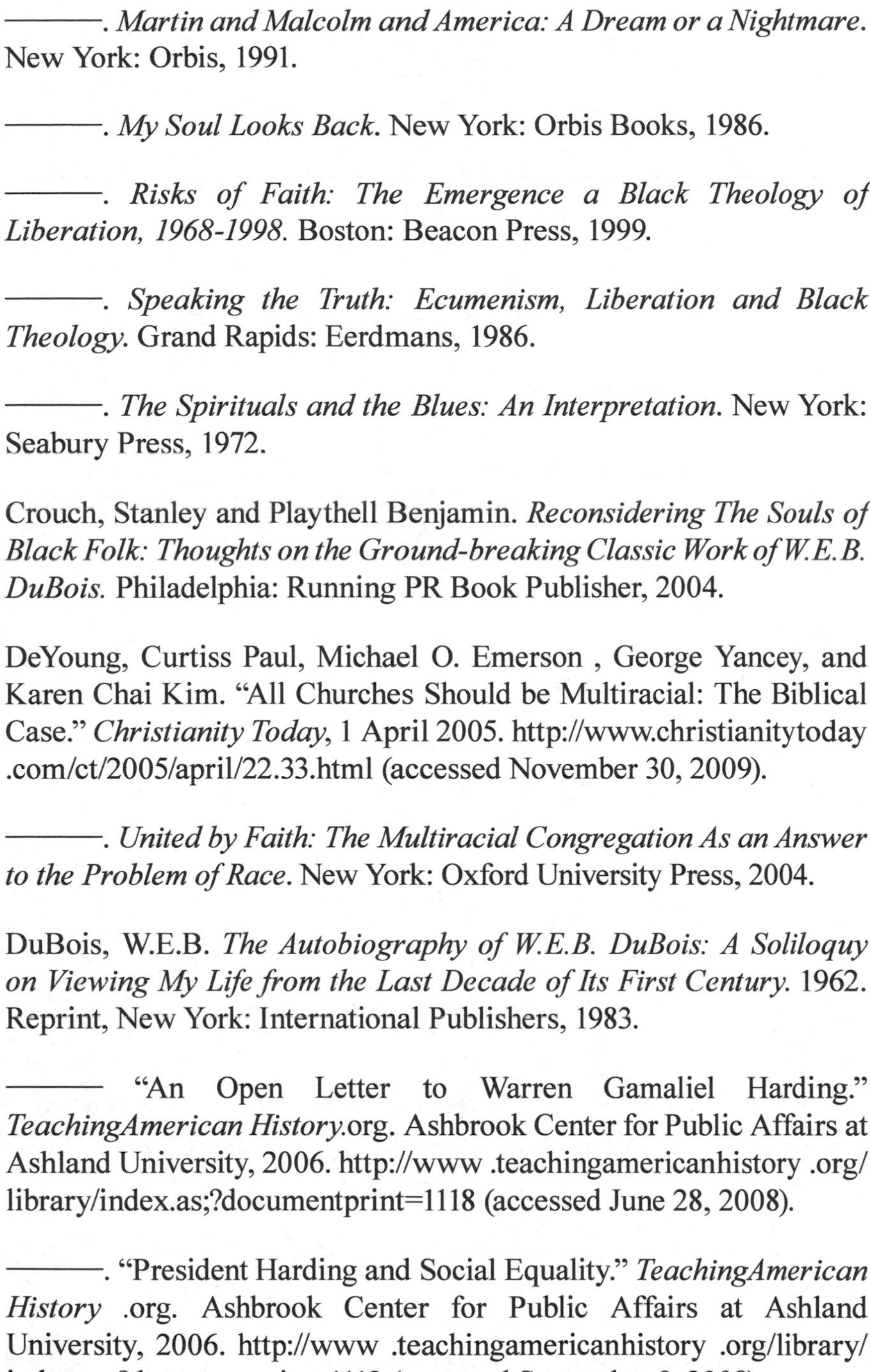

———. *Martin and Malcolm and America: A Dream or a Nightmare.* New York: Orbis, 1991.

———. *My Soul Looks Back.* New York: Orbis Books, 1986.

———. *Risks of Faith: The Emergence a Black Theology of Liberation, 1968-1998.* Boston: Beacon Press, 1999.

———. *Speaking the Truth: Ecumenism, Liberation and Black Theology.* Grand Rapids: Eerdmans, 1986.

———. *The Spirituals and the Blues: An Interpretation.* New York: Seabury Press, 1972.

Crouch, Stanley and Playthell Benjamin. *Reconsidering The Souls of Black Folk: Thoughts on the Ground-breaking Classic Work of W.E.B. DuBois.* Philadelphia: Running PR Book Publisher, 2004.

DeYoung, Curtiss Paul, Michael O. Emerson , George Yancey, and Karen Chai Kim. "All Churches Should be Multiracial: The Biblical Case." *Christianity Today*, 1 April 2005. http://www.christianitytoday .com/ct/2005/april/22.33.html (accessed November 30, 2009).

———. *United by Faith: The Multiracial Congregation As an Answer to the Problem of Race.* New York: Oxford University Press, 2004.

DuBois, W.E.B. *The Autobiography of W.E.B. DuBois: A Soliloquy on Viewing My Life from the Last Decade of Its First Century.* 1962. Reprint, New York: International Publishers, 1983.

——— "An Open Letter to Warren Gamaliel Harding." *TeachingAmerican History*.org. Ashbrook Center for Public Affairs at Ashland University, 2006. http://www .teachingamericanhistory .org/ library/index.as;?documentprint=1118 (accessed June 28, 2008).

———. "President Harding and Social Equality." *TeachingAmerican History* .org. Ashbrook Center for Public Affairs at Ashland University, 2006. http://www .teachingamericanhistory .org/library/ index.as;?documentprint=1118 (accessed September 9, 2008).

———. "W.E.B. DuBois Critiques Booker T. Washington." History Matters: The US Survey Course on the Web. American Social History Project / Center for Media and Learning (Graduate Center, CUNY) and the Center for History and New Media (George Mason University). http://historymatters.gmu.edu/d/40 (accessed September 3, 2008).

Dulles, Avery. *Models of the Church.* New York: Doubleday, 1978.

Emerson, Michael O. and Christian Smith. *Divided by Faith: Evangelical Religion and the Problem of Race in America.* New York: Oxford University Press, 2001.

Fleming, Walter L. *Documentary History of Reconstruction: Political, Military, Social, Religious, Educational & Industrial: 1865 to the Present Time*. 2 vols. Cleveland: The Arthur H. Clark Company, 1906-07.

Gibbs, Eddie. *Church Next: Quantum Changes in How We Do Ministry.* Downers Grove, IL: InterVarsity Press, 2000.

Gilbreath, Edward. Reconciliation Blues: A Black Evangelical's Inside View of White Christianity. Downers Grove, IL: InterVarsity Press, 2008.

Gingrich, F. Wilbur. *Shorter Lexicon of the Greek New Testament.* Chicago: University of Chicago Press, 1971.

Ginsberg, Morris. *On Justice in Society.* Ithaca, NY: Cornell University Press, 1965.

Gooding-Williams, Robert. *In the Shadow of Du Bois: Afro-Modern Political Thought in America.* (Cambridge: Harvard University Press, 2009).

Gordon, Wayne L. *Real Hope in Chicago*. Grand Rapids: Zondervan, 1995.

Gossett, Thomas F. *Race: The History of an Idea in America.* New York: Oxford University Press, 1997.

Graham, Billy. "Racism and the Evangelical Church." *Christianity Today,* 4 October 1993.

Gustafson, James. *Christian Ethics and the Community.* Philadelphia: Pilgrim Press, 1971.

———. *Ethics from a Theocentric Perspective.* Chicago: University of Chicago Press, 1981.

Hannaford, Ivan. *Race: The History of an Idea in the West.* Baltimore: Johns Hopkins University Press, 1996.

Harder, Gunther. *The International Dictionary of New Testament Theology.* Edited by Colin Brown. Grand Rapids: Zondervan, 1976.

Haugen, Gary A. *Good News about Injustice: A Witness of Courage in a Hurting World.* Downers Grove, IL: InterVarsity Press, 1999.

Henry, Carl F. H. *The Uneasy Conscience of Modern Fundamentalism.* Grand Rapids: Eerdmans, 2003.

Hopkins, Dwight N. *Being Human: Race, Culture, and Religion.* Minneapolis: Fortress, 2005.

———. *Black Theology of Liberation.* New York: Orbis, 1999.

Huggins, Nathan. *DuBois: Writings.* Library of America College eds. New York: The Library of America, 1986.

Jones, Major J. *Christian Ethics for Black Theology.* Nashville: Abingdon, 1974.

Keener, Craig S. *The IVP Bible Background Commentary: New Testament.* Downers Grove, IL: InterVarsity Press, 1993.

Keil, C. F. and F. Delitzsch. *Commentary on the Old Testament.* 10 vols. Grand Rapids: Eerdmans, 1976.

Kelly, Erin, ed. *Justice as Fairness: A Restatement*. Cambridge: Harvard University Press, 2001.

Lebacqz, Karen. *Six Theories of Justice*. Minneapolis: Augsburg, 1986.

Lenski, R. C. H. *The Interpretation of St. Paul's Epistles to Galatians, Ephesians and Philippians.* Minneapolis, MN: Augsburg, 1937.

Lewis, David Levering. *W.E.B. Du Bois: The Fight for Equality and the American Century, 1919-1963*. New York: Holt, 2001.

Lewis, Robert, Wayne Cordeiro, and Warren Bird. *Culture Shift: Transforming Your Church from the Inside Out*. San Francisco: Jossey-Bass, 2005.

Liefeld, Walter L. "Notes on Ephesians." *The NIV Study Bible: New International Version*. Edited by Kenneth L. Barker. Grand Rapids: Zondervan, 1985.

Lincoln, C. Eric. *Race, Religion, and the Continuing American Dilemma*. New York: Hill and Wang, 1999.

Loury, Glenn C., ed. *One by One from the Inside Out: Essays and Reviews on Race and Responsibility in America*. New York: The Free Press, 1995.

MacIntyre, Alasdair. *Ethics: A History of Moral Philosophy from the Homeric Age to the Twentieth Century*. New York: Touchstone, 1966.

Marsden, George M. *Fundamentalism and American Culture: The Shaping of Twentieth-Century Evangelicalism: 1870-1925*. New York: Oxford Press, 1980.

Martyn, J. Louis. "Apocalyptic Antinomies in Paul's Letter to the Galatians." *New Testament Studies* 31 (1985).

Mathews, Basil. *Booker T. Washington: Educator and Interracial Interpreter.* Cambridge: Harvard University Press, 1948.

McManus, Erwin R. *An Unstoppable Force: Daring to Become the Church God Had in Mind.* Loveland, CO: Group Publishing, 2001.

Meeks, Douglas M. and Robert D. Mutton, eds. *In Essentials Unity: Reflections on the Nature and Purpose of the Church.* Minneapolis: Kirk House, 2001.

Meier, August. *Negro Thought in America, 1880-1915: Racial Ideologies in the Age of Booker T. Washington.* Ann Arbor, MI: The University of Michigan Press, 1964.

Moltmann, Jürgen. *The Church in the Power of the Spirit.* London: SCM Press Ltd., 1977.

Montagu, Ashley. *Man's Most Dangerous Myth: The Fallacy of Race.* 5th ed. London: Oxford University Press, 1974.

———. 6th ed. Walnut Creek, CA: AltaMira, 1997.

Niebuhr, Reinhold. *Love and Justice: Selections from the Shorter Writings of Reinhold Niebuhr.* Edited by D. B. Robertson. Louisville, KY: Westminster Press, 1957.

———. *Moral Man and Immoral Society: A Study in Ethics and Politics.* Louisville: Westminster/John Knox Press, 2001.

Niebuhr, H. Richard. *Christ and Culture.* San Francisco: Harper, 1951.

Norrell, Robert J. *Up from History: The Life of Booker T. Washington.* Cambridge: Belknap Press of Harvard University Press, 2009.

Nygren, Anders. *Agape and Eros: A Study of the Christian Idea of Love.* Philadelphia: Westminster Press, 1953.

Outlaw, Lucius T. Jr. "On Cornel West on W.E.B. DuBois." In *Cornel West: A Critical Reader*, edited by George Yancy. London: Blackwell Publishers, 2001.

PBS. *Race: The Power of an Illusion. PBS*. Executive producer Larry Adelman. California Newsreel: 2003. http://www.pbs.org/race/000 About/002 04-background-01-11.htm (accessed July 27, 2008).

Perkins, John M. Beyond Charity: The Call to Christian Community Development. Grand Rapids: Baker, 1993.

———. Friday Morning Bible Study. Audio recording on *UrbanMinistry.org* , CCDA, 2005. www.urbanministry.org/audio/by/artist/john_perkins.html (accessed, February 2007).

———. Saturday Morning Bible Study. Audio recording on *UrbanMinistry.org*, CCDA, 2006. www.urbanministry.org/audio/by/artist/john_perkins.html (accessed February 2007).

———. Friday Morning Bible Study. Audio recording on YouTube, CCDA,1998. www.youtube.com/watch?v=QVDf9TUK9xM (accessed, February 2007).

———. *Let Justice Roll Down*. 1976. Reprint, Grand Rapids: Regal Books, 2006.

———. A Quiet Revolution: Meeting Human Needs Today: A Biblical Challenge to Christians. Rev. ed. Waco, TX: Waco Books, 1976.

———. *Restoring At Risk Communities: Doing It Together and Doing It Right*. Grand Rapids: Baker, 1995.

———. With Justice for All: A Strategy for Community Development. Grand Rapids: Regal Books, 2007.

Perkins, John M. and Gordon D. Aeschliman. *Land Where My Father Died*. Grand Rapids: Regal Books, 1987.

Perkins, John M., Ronald J. Sider, Wayne L. Gordon, and F. Albert Tizon. *Linking Arms, Linking Lives: How Urban-Suburban Partnerships Can Transform Communities.* Grand Rapids: Baker Books, 2008.

Perkins, John M. and Thomas A. Tarrants III. *He's My Brother.* Grand Rapids: Chosen Books, 1994.

Pinn, Anthony B. Moral Evil and Redemptive Suffering: A History of Theodicy in African-American Religious Thought. Gainesville, FL: University Press of Florida, 2002.

Rae, Scott B. *Moral Choices: An Introduction to Ethics.* Grand Rapids: Zondervan, 1993.

Rauschenbusch, Walter. *A Theology for the Social Gospel.* Louisville, KY: Westminster Press, 1945.

Rawls, John. *A Theory of Justice.* Cambridge: Harvard University Press, 1999.

Roberts, J. Deotis. Afrocentric Christianity: A Theological Appraisal for Ministry. Valley Forge, PA: Judson Press, 2000.

———. *A Black Political Theology.* Philadelphia: Westminster Press, 1974.

———. *Black Religion, Black Theology: The Collected Essays of J. Deotis Roberts.* New York: Trinity Press International, 2003.

———. *Black Theology in Dialogue.* Philadelphia: Westminster Press, 1987.

———. *Black Theology Today.* Lewiston, NY: Edwin Mellen Press, 1984.

———. *Bonhoeffer and King: Speaking Truth to Power.* Louisville, KY: Westminster/John Knox Press, 2005.

———. *Christian Beliefs*, 3rd ed. Silver Spring, MD: The J. Deotis Roberts Press, 2000.

———. "Contextual Theology: Liberation and Indigenization." *ChickenBones: A Journal for Literary and Artistic African American Themes*. http://nathanielturner.com/ contextualtheology.htm (accessed August 24, 2008). Also available in print version: *The Christian Century* (January 28, 1976).

———. *Faith and Reason in Pascal, Bergson and James*. Boston: Christopher Publishing House, 1962.

———. From Puritanism to Platonism in Seventeenth Century England. The Hague: Martinus Nijhoff, 1968.

———. *Liberation and Reconciliation*. Rev. ed. New York: Orbis Books, 1994.

———. *A Philosophical Introduction to Theology*. Philadelphia: Trinity Press International, 1991.

———. *The Prophethood of Black Believers: An African American Political Theology for Ministry*. Louisville, KY: Westminster/John Knox Press, 1994.

———. *Roots of a Black Future: Family and Church*. Philadelphia: Westminster Press, 1980.

Roberts, J. Deotis and Michael Battle, eds. *The Quest for Liberation and Reconciliation: Essays in Honor of J. Deotis Roberts*. Louisville, KY: Westminster/John Knox Press, 2005.

Roberts, J. Deotis and James Gardiner. *Quest for a Black Theology*. Philadelphia: Pilgrim Press, 1971.

Robinson, Anthony B. *Transforming Congregational Culture*. Grand Rapids: Eerdmans Publishing, 2003.

Roucek, J. S. and T. P. Kiernan, eds. *The Negro Impact on Western Civilization.* New York: Philosophical Library, 1970.

Rudwick, Elliott M. *W.E.B. Du Bois: Propagandist of the Negro Protest.* New York: Atheneum, 1960.

Sanders, Cheryl J. *Empowerment Ethics for a Liberated People: A Path to African American Social Transformation.* Minneapolis, MN: Fortress Press, 1995.

Schaeffer, Francis A. *The Complete Works of Francis Schaeffer: A Christian Worldview.* Vol. 5 of A Christian View of the West. Wheaton, IL: Crossway Books, 1996.

Sidgwick, Henry. *The Methods of Ethics.* London: MacMillan, 1907.

Stackhouse, John Gordon, ed. *Evangelical Ecclesiology: Reality or Illusion?* Grand Rapids: Baker Academic, 2003.

Stassen, Glen H. and David P. Gushee. *Kingdom Ethics: Following Jesus in Contemporary Context.* Downers Grove, IL: InterVarsity Press, 2003.

Steele, Shelby. *The Content of Our Character: A New Vision of Race in America.* New York: Harper Collins, 1991.

Sterne, Emma Gelders. *His Was The Voice: The Life of W.E.B. DuBois.* New York: Crowell-Collier Press, 1971.

Stott, John R. W. *Christian Mission in the Modern World.* Downers Grove, IL: InterVarsity Press, 1975.

Sundquist, Eric J., ed. *The Oxford W.E.B. DuBois Reader.* New York: Oxford University Press, 1996.

———. "W.E.B. DuBois: Up To Slavery." *Commentary* (December 1986): 62-67.

Tapia, Andres. "The Myth of Racial Progress." *Christianity Today*, 4 October 1993.

Taylor, Quintard, ed. *African American History of Western New York.* http://www.math.buffalo.edu/~sww/0history/hwny-niagara-movement.html (accessed June 28, 2008).

*Theological Wordbook of the Old Testament.* Edited by R. Laird Harris, Gleason L. Archer, Jr., and Bruce K. Waltke. Chicago: Moody Press, 1980.

Thomson, John B. *The Ecclesiology of Stanley Hauerwas: A Christian Theology of Liberation.* Burlington, VT: Ashgate Publishing, 2003.

Troeltsch, Ernst. *The Social Teachings of the Christian Church.* New York: Macmillan, 1931.

Veli-Matti, Karkainnen. *An Introduction to Ecclesiology: Ecumenical Historical and Global Perspectives.* Downers Grove, IL: InterVarsity Press, 2002.

Volf, Miroslav. *After Our Likeness: The Church as the Image of the Trinity.* Grand Rapids, MI: Eerdmans Publishing, 1998.

Wallace, Robert, "A Racialized Medical Genomics: Shiny, Bright and Wrong." In *Race: The Power of an Illusion*, "Background Readings." *PBS*. California Newsreel: 2003. http://www.pbs.org/race/000_About/002_04-background-01-13.htm (accessed August11, 2008).

Wallis, Jim. God's Politics: Why the Right Gets It Wrong and the Left Doesn't Get it. San Francisco: HarperCollins, 2005.

Walzer, Michael. *Spheres of Justice*. New York: Basic Books, 1983.

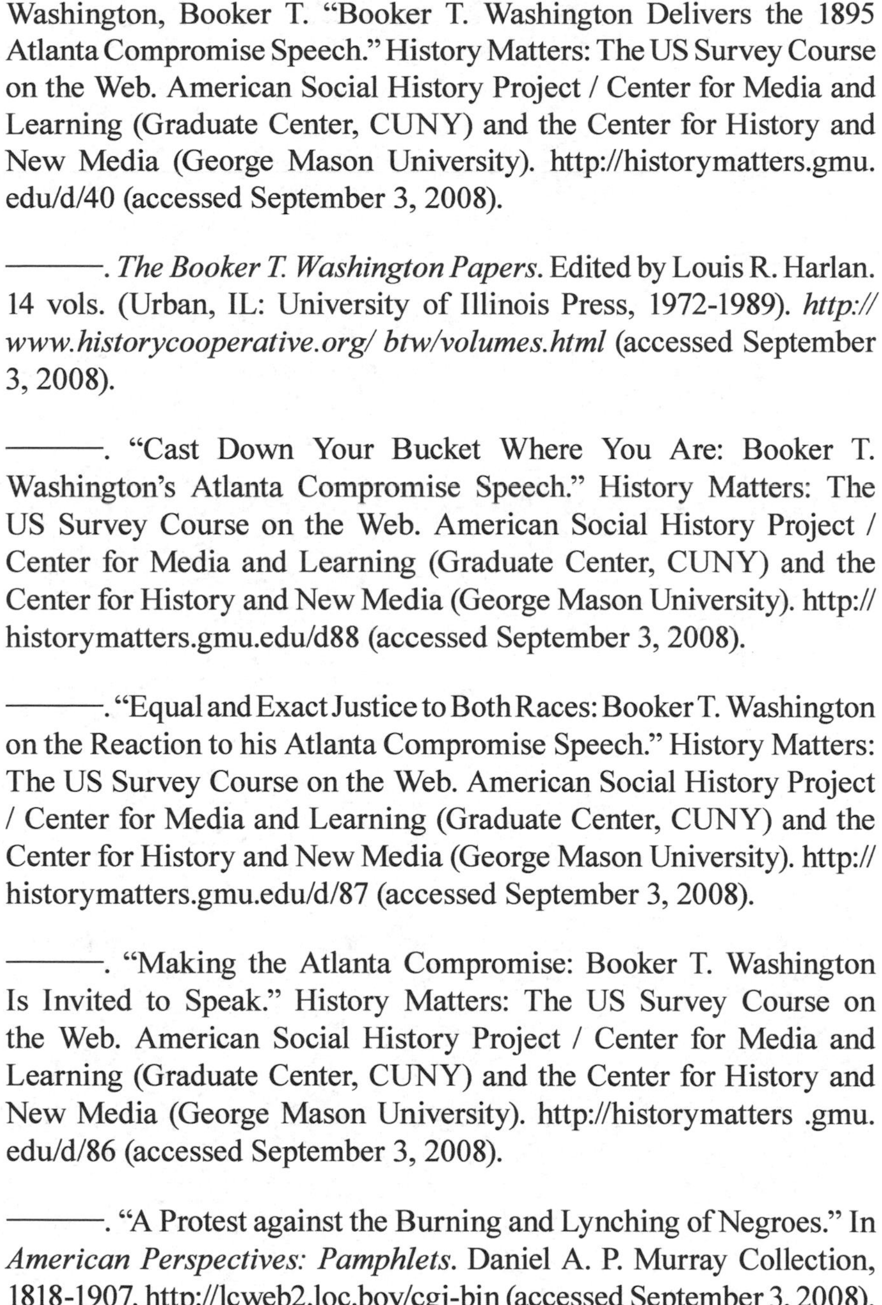

Washington, Booker T. “Booker T. Washington Delivers the 1895 Atlanta Compromise Speech.” History Matters: The US Survey Course on the Web. American Social History Project / Center for Media and Learning (Graduate Center, CUNY) and the Center for History and New Media (George Mason University). http://historymatters.gmu.edu/d/40 (accessed September 3, 2008).

———. *The Booker T. Washington Papers*. Edited by Louis R. Harlan. 14 vols. (Urban, IL: University of Illinois Press, 1972-1989). *http://www.historycooperative.org/ btw/volumes.html* (accessed September 3, 2008).

———. “Cast Down Your Bucket Where You Are: Booker T. Washington’s Atlanta Compromise Speech.” History Matters: The US Survey Course on the Web. American Social History Project / Center for Media and Learning (Graduate Center, CUNY) and the Center for History and New Media (George Mason University). http://historymatters.gmu.edu/d88 (accessed September 3, 2008).

———. “Equal and Exact Justice to Both Races: Booker T. Washington on the Reaction to his Atlanta Compromise Speech.” History Matters: The US Survey Course on the Web. American Social History Project / Center for Media and Learning (Graduate Center, CUNY) and the Center for History and New Media (George Mason University). http://historymatters.gmu.edu/d/87 (accessed September 3, 2008).

———. “Making the Atlanta Compromise: Booker T. Washington Is Invited to Speak.” History Matters: The US Survey Course on the Web. American Social History Project / Center for Media and Learning (Graduate Center, CUNY) and the Center for History and New Media (George Mason University). http://historymatters .gmu.edu/d/86 (accessed September 3, 2008).

———. “A Protest against the Burning and Lynching of Negroes.” In *American Perspectives: Pamphlets*. Daniel A. P. Murray Collection, 1818-1907. http://lcweb2.loc.bov/cgi-bin (accessed September 3, 2008).

———. “Up From Slavery.” *Commentary* (December 1986).

Watson, Natalie. *Introducing Feminine Ecclesiology*. Edited by Mary Gray, Lisa Isherwood and Janet Wootten. Philadelphia: Pilgrim Press, 2002.

West, Cornel. *Prophesy Deliverance: An Afro-American Revolutionary Christianity*. Louisville, KY: Westminster John Knox Press, 1982.

———. *Race Matters*. New York: Vintage Books, 1993.

Wilmore, Gayraud. Black Religion and Black Radicalism: An Interpretation of the Religious History of African Americans. 3rd ed. New York: Orbis, 2003.

———. *Last Things First (Library of Living Faith)*. Philadelphia: Westminster Press, 1982.

———. *Pragmatic Spirituality: The Christian Faith through an Africentric Lens*. New York: University Press, 2004.

———. *The Secular Relevance of the Church*. Philadelphia: Westminster Press, 1962.

Wilmore, Gayraud and Beth Basham. *Black and Presbyterian: The Heritage and the Hope*. Louisville, KY: Westminster/John Knox Press, 1998.

Wilmore, Gayraud S. and James H. Cone, eds. *Black Theology: A Documentary History, 1966-1979*. Maryknoll, NY: Orbis, 1979.

———. Rev. ed. New York: Orbis, 1993.

———, eds. *Black Theology: A Documented History*. Vol. 2 of *1980-1992*. Rev. ed. New York: Orbis, 1993.

Wilmore, Gayraud S. and David T. Shannon, eds. *Black Witness to the Apostolic Faith*. Grand Rapids: Eerdmans Publishing, 1985.

Wilmore, Gayraud and Eugene G. Turner. *Dissent and Empowerment: Essays in Honor of Gayraud S. Wilmore*. Louisville, KY: Westminster/ John Knox Press, 1999.

Witzig, Ritchie. "The Medicalization of Race: Scientific Legitimization of a Flawed Social Construct." *Annals of Internal Medicine* 125 (1996), http://annals.highwire.org/ cgi/content/full/125/8/675 (accessed August 11, 2008).

Wood, A. Skevington. "Ephesians." *The Expositor's Bible Commentary: Ephesians through Philemon*. Edited by Frank E. Gaebelein. Grand Rapids: Zondervan, 1978.

Yoder, Perry B. *Shalom: The Bible's Word for Salvation, Justice and Peace*. Newton, KS: Faith and Life Press, 1987.

wed thu
thu – fri 10 – 8 am
fri sat
Sat – Sunday — 10 pm – 8 am
Sun Mon – 10 pm – 8 am
Mon – Tue – 10 pm – 7 am
Tue – wed 10 pm – 8 am
thursday
Friday